North Carolina

BED & BREAKFAST

Cookbook

3D PRESS
BOULDER

ISBN 978-1-889593-28-9
PRINTED IN China
COVER AND TEXT DESIGN: Rebecca Finkel
COMPOSITION: Kari Luraas
EDITOR: Mira Perrizo

FRONT COVER PHOTO: Inn At Iris Meadows
BACK COVER PHOTOS: Peaches in Orange Sauce in a Puff Pancake from
A Bed of Roses, Victorian B&B; Beaufort House Inn

3D Press, Inc.
3360 Mitchell Lane, Suite E
Boulder, CO 80301
800-258-5830 (order toll-free)
info@bigearthpublishing.com (email)
www.bigearthpublishing.com

The Bed & Breakfast Cookbook Series was originated by Carol Faino and Doreen Hazledine of Peppermint Press in Denver, CO in 1999.

DISCLAIMER AND LIMITS OF LIABILITY

Contents

North Carolina

In 1585, Sir Walter Raleigh sent English colonists to settle on Roanoke Island in the northeast corner of North Carolina. The first American child of English parentage, Virginia Dare, was born there. When a relief expedition arrived in 1591, everyone had disappeared, and the "lost colony" is a mystery that remains today.

North Carolina saw little fighting in the state during the Civil War, but her soldiers fought for the Confederacy with such fierceness that they earned the nickname Tar Heels, since the troops "stuck to their ranks like they had tar on their heels." At least that's one story. It has become the moniker for the University of North Carolina athletic teams, students, alumni, and fans.

Washington Duke's successful tobacco enterprise gave birth to another well-known university, Duke, located in Durham. Our early economy included furniture, textiles, and tobacco. Though today the state's major agricultural products are tobacco, corn, cotton, hay, and peanuts, North Carolina has flourished and grown with knowledge-based enterprises such as biotechnology, pharmaceuticals, and life sciences. The state was ranked the third best state for business in 2010 by *Forbes* magazine.

Another huge industry is tourism, with over $1 billion spent annually in the state. Because of our diverse topography, from the mountains, through the piedmont, to the shore, many sports are available year-round, including golfing, skiing at mountain resorts, both fresh- and salt-water fishing, and hunting.

Discover North Carolina anew by visiting our member B&Bs and Inns throughout the state. Experience our Southern hospitality, intriguing history, and mouth-watering cuisine. So much to enjoy!

State Symbols

State Bird: Cardinal

State Flower: Dogwood

State Tree: Pine

State Insect: Honeybee

State Mammal: Gray Squirrel

State Fruit: Scuppernong grape

State Gemstone: Emerald

State Motto: *Esse quam videri*

    (To be rather than to seem)

Famous North Carolinians

Dolly Madison

James K. Polk

Andrew Johnson

Richard Petty

Edward R. Murrow

Andy Griffith

O. Henry

Thomas Wolfe

Thelonious Monk

Floyd Patterson

Billy Graham

Ava Gardner

Earl Scruggs

James Taylor

Darryl Moran Photography

Fun Facts about North Carolina

- Pepsi Cola was founded in New Bern in 1902.

- The Pinehurst Number 2, completed in 1907, is the site of two US Open championships. North Carolina is one of the 5 most popular states for golfers.

- The Charlotte Mint, branch of the U.S. Mint, came into existence on March 3, 1835, during the Carolina Gold Rush.

- Salem was founded in 1766 by the Moravians, a Protestant group from the area now known as the Czech Republic. The Moravian missionaries established the 100,000-acre tract of "Wachovia."

- The Wright brothers completed the first successful flight of a mechanically propelled airplane over the sands of Kitty Hawk, on December 17, 1903.

- Babe Ruth hit his first professional home run in Fayetteville on March 7, 1914.

- The Biltmore Estate is the largest private house in the world, with 250 rooms.

- Albemarle Sound is the largest freshwater sound in the world.

- The Cape Hatteras Lighthouse is the tallest lighthouse in the U.S.

- Because of the bombing of Pearl Harbor on December 7, 1941, the Rose Bowl was not played in Pasadena, California, but in Durham, North Carolina. Duke, who had already been invited to play, volunteered to host the game. On a cold, rainy January 1, 1942, Duke lost to Oregon State, 20–16.

Introduction

Looking for a good recipe? Take a cup of the stunning view from the Blue Ridge Parkway and the Great Smoky Mountains. Add large spoonfuls of sun-kissed sand from the seashore, along with a basketful of the sounds of shorebirds. Mix in a pinch of the scent of dogwoods and roses from the Sarah Duke Gardens. Season with the crack of a baseball bat, the swing of a golf club, or the swoosh of a pair of skis. Serve with the beautiful and diverse arts, crafts, and music for which our state is renowned.

Our innkeepers offer gorgeous accommodations in scenic, diverse, and exciting areas to explore, play, and relax in. Now they are generously sharing their favorite recipes to satisfy all of your senses. The variety revealed in these recipes is a hint of the range of style in our North Carolina Bed & Breakfasts and Inns Association members.

These recipes run the gamut from the most simple, elegant breakfast dish to fabulous entrées for elaborate dinners. You'll find recipes for a holiday punch that refreshes the multitudes, as well as yummy desserts to adorn your table, if you can get them to the table before they are eaten—soft, warm and oh-so-delicious from the oven.

Our innkeepers invite you to indulge in a taste of North Carolina. Our cookbook represents the best of the best, in taste, flavor, appearance, and appeal. Once you try these recipes, the experience will assure that you never forget the absolute deliciousness of North Carolina hospitality! It will become part of your life, as it has with us. The recipes are tried and true and the most requested from our guests. So take a plunge into this cookbook, and get out the flour, butter, and mixing bowls. Indulge your basic need to feed your family and friends!

When you are ready to relax and pamper yourself, consider the comfort of one of our member inns. Our members tell you a bit about themselves in the front of this cookbook, just a tease at the potential of each, all served up with a hearty dollop of gracious southern hospitality.

Visit www.ncbbi.org to find out more.

Debbie Vickery
President, North Carolina Bed & Breakfasts and Inns

U.S. Measurement Equivalents

pinch/dash	$1/16$ teaspoon
½ teaspoon	30 drops
1 teaspoon	$1/3$ tablespoon
3 teaspoons	1 tablespoon
½ tablespoon	1½ teaspoons
1 tablespoon	3 teaspoons; ½ fluid ounce
2 tablespoons	$1/8$ cup; 1 fluid ounce
3 tablespoons	1½ fluid ounces; 1 jigger
jigger	1½ fluid ounces; 3 tablespoons
4 tablespoons	¼ cup; 2 fluid ounces
5$1/3$ tablespoons	$1/3$ cup; 5 tablespoons + 1 teaspoon
8 tablespoons	½ cup; 4 fluid ounces
10$2/3$ tablespoons	$2/3$ cup; 10 tablespoons + 2 teaspoons
12 tablespoons	¾ cup; 6 fluid ounces
16 tablespoons	1 cup; 8 fluid ounces; ½ pint
$1/8$ cup	2 tablespoons; 1 fluid ounce
¼ cup	4 tablespoons; 2 fluid ounces
$1/3$ cup	5 tablespoons + 1 teaspoon
$3/8$ cup	¼ cup + 2 tablespoons
½ cup	8 tablespoons; 4 fluid ounces
$2/3$ cup	10 tablespoons + 2 teaspoons
$5/8$ cup	½ cup + 2 tablespoons
¾ cup	12 tablespoons; 6 fluid ounces
$7/8$ cup	¾ cup + 2 tablespoons
1 cup	16 tablespoons; ½ pint; 8 fluid ounces
2 cups	1 pint; 16 fluid ounces
3 cups	1½ pints; 24 fluid ounces
4 cups	1 quart; 32 fluid ounces
8 cups	2 quarts; 64 fluid ounces
1 pint	2 cups; 16 fluid ounces
2 pints	1 quart; 32 fluid ounces
1 quart	2 pints; 4 cups; 32 fluid ounces
4 quarts	1 gallon; 8 pints
1 gallon	4 quarts; 8 pints; 16 cups; 128 fluid ounces
8 quarts	1 peck
4 pecks	1 bushel

Geographical Listing of Bed & Breakfasts

North Carolina

BED & BREAKFAST

Establishments
and their Signature Recipes

1889 WhiteGate Inn & Cottage

INNKEEPERS	Ralph Coffey & Frank Salvo
ADDRESS	173 East Chestnut Street, Asheville, NC 28801
TELEPHONE	828-253-2553 | 800-485-3045
CONTACT	innkeeper@whitegate.net | www.whitegate.net
FEATURES	2 Rooms; 8 Suites; 1 Cottage | Private Baths | Children welcome | Dogs allowed (Limited suites) | Full ADA handicap suite (including parking) | Will accommodate guests' special dietary needs

Romance, elegance, and tranquility describe the ambiance at the 1889 WhiteGate Inn & Cottage. This charming Four Diamond Award winning, Select Registry B&B in Asheville is listed on the National Register of Historic Places. Sumptuous breakfasts begin your day. Luxurious spa suites with two-person Jacuzzi tubs and fireplaces set the tone for romance. Wander the stunning award-winning gardens or stroll to shops and restaurants in Asheville, less than a five-minute walk away.

Choose between 3 luxury suites located in the Carriage House and enjoy the ultimate in luxurious accommodations. The Bungalow consists of 2 suites complete with full kitchens and Jacuzzi tubs, which can be combined to create a 3-bedroom, full-house rental. This delightful pet friendly B&B is perfect for families traveling with children and

dogs. The award-winning gardens have an extensive collection of unusual plants. The greenhouse has a collection of over 1,000 orchids and tropicals. Paths and sitting areas throughout the gardens make it a perfect place to wander or to sit and meditate.

Asparagus & Herb Egg Bake

Yield: 18 servings

36	eggs (2 eggs per person)
3	cups milk
1	tsp salt
1	tsp pepper
2	tsp dried oregano
2	tsp dried rosemary
2	tsp dried chives
1–1½	lbs. fresh asparagus, cut into 1 inch pieces
3	cups shredded cheddar cheese
16	oz. cottage cheese
8	oz. cream cheese, cubed

In a bowl, beat together eggs and milk. Add all other ingredients and pour into a 10x15x2-inch baking dish. Cover with plastic wrap and refrigerate overnight. Preheat oven to 400°F. Remove pan from refrigerator and bake for 20 minutes.

1898 WAVERLY INN

INNKEEPERS	John & Diane Sheiry and Darla Olmstead
ADDRESS	783 North Main Street, Hendersonville, NC 28792
TELEPHONE	828-693-9193	800-537-8195
CONTACT	info@waverlyinn.com	www.waverlyinn.com
FEATURES	14 Rooms and 1 Suite; Private baths	Children welcome	1 pet friendly room	Will accommodate guests' special dietary needs

The 1898 Waverly Inn offers comfortable accommodations, modern amenities, and outstanding customer service. Conveniently located in historic Downtown Hendersonville, the Inn offers easy access to fabulous restaurants, unique shops, and galleries. Hendersonville is centrally located to many of western North Carolina's most loved attractions. The staff is always eager to offer suggestions and maps for things to do in the area.

The 1898 Waverly Inn is known for its wonderful, cooked to order, farm-to-table breakfast and Darla's homemade cookies and cake. Join the Innkeepers each evening from 5–6 p.m. for tasting hour. Come experience hospitality as it was meant to be.

Apple Cake
Yield: 12 servings

Raw sugar (natural sugar)
1½ cups all-purpose flour
 1 cup packed brown sugar
 1 tsp cinnamon
 ½ tsp nutmeg
 1 tsp salt
 1 tsp baking soda
 1 tsp baking powder
 1 stick butter, melted and cooled
 ½ cup vegetable oil
 3 large eggs
 ¾ cup orange juice
Powdered sugar, for garnish (optional)

Apple topping:
 1 large Granny Smith apple, thinly sliced
 1 stick butter, melted and cooled
 1 tsp cinnamon
 ¼ cup all-purpose flour

Preheat oven to 350°F. Spray a Bundt pan with non-stick cooking spray and sprinkle with raw sugar. In a large bowl, combine flour, brown sugar, cinnamon, nutmeg, salt, baking soda and baking powder. In a medium bowl, combine butter, oil, eggs and orange juice; add to flour mixture and stir to combine. For the apple topping: In a small bowl, combine apples, butter, cinnamon and flour; toss to coat apples well.

Pour batter into pan. Arrange apple topping over batter. Bake for 40–45 minutes, or until a toothpick inserted in center comes out clean. Cool cake, then dust with powdered sugar, if desired.

803 ELIZABETH B&B

INNKEEPERS	Martha & Will Krauss
ADDRESS	803 Elizabeth Lane, Matthews NC 28105
TELEPHONE	704-841-8900 | Fax 704-847-5094
CONTACT	Martha@803elizabeth.com | www.803elizabeth.com
FEATURES	3 rooms; 2 Private baths; 1 shared bath | Children age 6 and older welcome | No pets, 2 resident outdoor cats | Will accommodate guests' special dietary needs

The 803 Elizabeth B&B is located on five acres of gardens and wooded areas. The inn is in a neighborhood in the town of Matthews, just 12 miles southeast of Charlotte.

The yard features seasonal gardens of flowers, herbs, vegetables, and fruits. Stroll through the gardens and you will find something in bloom every day of the year.

"803 Elizabeth Lane soon becomes a lovely name
Delicious breakfast starts your day and makes you happy any way
Is really magic this wonderful place,
great comes a smile upon your face. Grazie di tottoo."
—Guests Antonella & Roberto

Frittata for 4

"This is a quick and easy recipe that you can finish in the oven. When the peppers are ripe in the garden, we cook the onions and peppers and freeze in ¼-cup batches."—Innkeeper

6 eggs
1 tsp water
4 drops red pepper sauce
2 tsp fresh mixed herbs—thyme, rosemary, sage

2 Tbsp chopped pepper (red green or yellow)
2 Tbsp chopped onion
3 Tbsp chopped ham
¼ cup grated cheddar cheese

Preheat oven to 400°F. In a bowl, whisk together the eggs, water, pepper sauce and herbs. Fry peppers and onions in an ovenproof frying pan until softened. Add ham then place mixture in a separate bowl. Pour egg mixture into frying pan, lifting sides gently with a spatula and cook until about half done. Spread pepper, onion and ham mixture onto the top of the eggs. Add grated cheese and place in oven until cheese melts and eggs are set. Slide onto a large round dinner plate, cut in quarters, and serve immediately.

1906 Pine Crest Inn & Restaurant

INNKEEPER	Carl Caudle
ADDRESS	85 Pine Crest Lane, Tryon, NC 28782
TELEPHONE	828-859-9135 | 800-633-3001
CONTACT	cooking@pinecrestinn.com | www.pinecrestinn.com
FEATURES	35 Rooms, Suites & Cottages, Private baths | Children welcome | Pets: Inquire

Looking for a B&B in western North Carolina? Imagine a 250-year-old romantic cabin so captivating that it inspired the writings of F. Scott Fitzgerald and Ernest Hemingway. Envision a relaxing evening on our verandas sipping tea or your favorite scotch from a collection of single-malts while watching the sun sink behind the beautiful Blue Ridge Mountains. Waterfall hikes, winery tours, intimate couples massage … these experiences and more can be found at this distinctive retreat nestled on 10 beautifully landscaped acres in historic Tryon.

The Inn is renowned for its "Best Breakfast in the Southeast," while Carter's Tavern & Wine Cellar offers casual fine dining focused on locally grown ingredients and fresh herbs from our organic gardens. Its wine list is the second largest in the Carolinas. The Fox & Hounds Bar features 32 different specialty beers and over 200 spirits. The inn has been recognized in *Southern Living, USA Today, Our State,* and *Fodor's,* and is listed on the National Historic Registry.

Sumptuous Stuffed French Toast

Yield: 4 servings

- 2 Tbsp unsalted butter
- 2 Tbsp dark brown sugar
- 2 Tbsp fresh orange juice
- 1 medium ripe banana, sliced into ¼-inch rounds
- 2 Tbsp Frangelico or dark rum
- 8 oz. cream cheese at room temperature
- 8 pieces Texas Toast or other thickly sliced bread
- 2 eggs, at room temperature
- ¼ cup sugar
- 2 cups half & half

- 1 Tbsp fresh orange zest
- ½ tsp freshly ground nutmeg
- 1 tsp vanilla

For Compote:
- 1 cup sliced peaches, plums or other stone fruit
- ½ cup berries (blue, black, straw, rasp)
- 2 Tbsp sugar
- 1 Tbsp fresh lemon juice
- ¼ cup water
- 1 Tbsp cornstarch

Prepare the fruit compote by peeling the stone fruit and slicing thinly into a heavy saucepan. Combine the fruit and berries with the sugar and lemon juice. Bring to a simmer and allow to reduce slightly. Combine water and cornstarch. Add to fruit mixture and allow compote to thicken slightly. If too thick, thin with water. Keep warm.

In a sauté pan, melt butter and brown sugar and stir in orange juice. Add sliced bananas and liquor and heat through. Allow to cool slightly and fold into cream cheese. This mixture can be made well in advance. Spread the Texas Toast with a generous portion of the cream cheese mixture and top with another slice of bread to make a sandwich. Trim the crust from the four edges and cut diagonally. Allow to rest on a wire rack for 10–15 minutes.

Whisk eggs, sugar, half & half, orange zest, nutmeg, and vanilla in a shallow dish. Heat lightly oiled griddle or pan to medium high heat. Dip triangles into egg mixture to coat thoroughly. Place the triangles onto the griddle and cook until golden on all sides and edges. Hold in a warm oven while preparing additional pieces. Place triangles on warm plates and top with fruit compote.

A Bed of Roses, Victorian B&B

INNKEEPERS	Bill and Emily McIntosh
ADDRESS	135 Cumberland Avenue, Asheville, NC 28801
TELEPHONE	828-258-8700 | 888-290-2770
CONTACT	stay@abedofroses.com | www.abedofroses.com
FEATURES	5 Rooms; 1 Suite; 5 Private baths | Children age 12 and older welcome | No pets, 2 resident cats | Will accommodate guests' special dietary needs

"Wow! What an amazing stay! Breakfast was wonderful (every morning) and the room was just what we needed—cozy and comfortable. We couldn't feel more at home during our weekend getaway. Thanks for making this weekend so special! We will definitely be back!—Guests Mike and Erin

A Bed of Roses is a romantic get-away, located in the charming historic Montford District, only 5 blocks from vibrant downtown Asheville. This precious Queen Anne Victorian was built in 1897 and has been fully restored to retain the Victorian elegance while providing all of the modern conveniences.

Set back from the tree-lined street, our shaded front porch provides a relaxing venue for enjoying the rose gardens or curling up with a good book or a glass of wine. The inn offers 5 antique-filled guest rooms with private baths, fireplaces, Jacuzzis, and free WiFi throughout. Breakfast is a special occasion, with a fruit course and a main course including side dishes, beautifully presented and delightfully delicious. We emphasize fresh local ingredients prepared with care and imagination.

Chorizo Frittata

Yield: 4 servings

6 oz. chorizo, sliced (or you can use the kind you crumble)
1 large red or Yukon gold potato
1 tsp olive oil
½ onion, diced
½ green pepper, diced
½ red pepper, diced (or 1 small jar roasted red pepper, drained and diced)

1 jalapeño (optional)
5 eggs
⅓ cup milk
¼ tsp cumin
¼ tsp oregano
¼ tsp sage
salt & pepper to taste
3 oz. grated Mexican cheese
3 tsp butter, divided

Slice and sauté chorizo, then quarter. (If using tube chorizo, crumble and sauté.) Remove from pan with a slotted spoon and reserve. Slice 1 large potato, red or Yukon gold, and steam for 7 minutes. Let cool. Preheat the deep part of the Frittata pan until rim is hot to the touch and add 1 teaspoon olive oil. Sauté onion, green and red pepper. Add chorizo and jalapeño to warm and transfer mixture to a medium bowl with the steamed potato. Whisk together the eggs, milk and spices in large bowl. Add the vegie-chorizo-potato mixture and the cheese.

Preheat deep part of Frittata pan again over medium heat and add 2 teaspoons butter. When foam subsides, add the egg mixture and cook about 10 minutes or until the eggs are set. (If using a deep ovenproof fry pan instead of a frittata pan, cover at this point). When eggs are set add 1 teaspoon butter to top pan and swirl. Interlock top to bottom and flip the pan. Cook 1 or 2 minutes longer. (In a regular ovenproof pan, transfer to the oven and broil just until the top is flaked with brown. Serve.) Flip the pan again, remove top and shake the frittata loose onto a serving plate or cutting board. Divide into 4 slices.

Garnish with a dollop of sour cream and cilantro. Serve with sliced tomato, green and yellow peppers, corn bread, and cilantro black bean and corn salsa. Can double in two pans.

ACORN B&B AT MILLS RIVER

INNKEEPERS	Gene Wyatt and Bob Pompeo
ADDRESS	5136 Old Haywood Road, Mills River, NC 28759
TELEPHONE	828-891-4652
CONTACT	innkeeper@acornbedbreakfast.com | www.acornbedbreakfast.com
FEATURES	4 Rooms; 2 Private baths, 2 Shared baths | Well-behaved children welcome | Dog guests welcome with previous arrangements (accommodations limited).

If you are looking for an Asheville B&B, consider Acorn B&B at Mills River, which is conveniently located between Asheville and Hendersonville, just minutes away from the Asheville Regional Airport. This cozy four-bedroom retreat offers guests a homelike atmosphere to relax and enjoy. Nestled in the foothills of the beautiful Blue Ridge Mountains, the Acorn B&B at Mills River is just a short drive to area attractions, including the Biltmore Estate, Western North Carolina Agricultural Center, Flat Rock Playhouse, and Chimney Rock Park.

Formally a private residence, the Acorn B&B was a dream of innkeepers Gene Wyatt and Bob Pompeo for many years. Gene has a degree in culinary arts and has worked for Carnival Cruise Lines and Biltmore Estate. Bob, a social worker by profession, also had the pleasure of working for the Disney Company. With their combined experiences they have created a "home away from home" lodging experience for their guests.

"We have transformed our home into a place where you can come for a relaxing experience away from the daily hustle and bustle, or for a place to hang your hat while you are climbing a mountain or going down the French Broad River on a raft."—Innkeepers

Cinnamon Pecan Stuffed French Toast

Yield: 8 servings

8–10 cups french bread cut into 1-inch cubes. Any combination of sweet breads/pastries may be used. We like to use leftover cinnamon rolls or cinnamon bread.
1 (8 oz.) pkg. cream cheese, cubed
½ cup pecans, whole or chopped (optional)
8 eggs
2½ cups milk (light cream or a combination)
½ cup white sugar
1 tsp vanilla
1 tsp baking powder
½ cup heavy cream for topping
½ cup white sugar mixed with 1 tsp cinnamon

12–24 hours before serving: Spray 9x13x2-inch pan with non-stick baking spray. Layer bread/pastry cubes in pan, sprinkle cubed cream cheese and pecans on top of mixture. In a large bowl, beat eggs, milk, sugar, vanilla and baking powder until well mixed. Pour over bread and cream cheese mixture and refrigerate until ready to bake. Preheat oven to 350°F. Pour ½ cup heavy cream over mixture and sprinkle with sugar/cinnamon mixture and bake for about 45 minutes or until a knife comes out clean. Serve with praline sauce.

Praline Sauce
½ lb. butter
2 lbs. light brown sugar
2 cups water
1 can sweetened condensed milk

Melt butter in a heavy saucepan. Add brown sugar and water. Cook until this mixture comes to a boil and cook for about 5 minutes. Add sweetened condensed milk and bring to another boil.

THE AERIE B&B, GUEST HOUSE AND CONFERENCE CENTER

INNKEEPERS	Marty & Michael Gunhus
ADDRESS	509 Pollock St, New Bern, NC 28562
TELEPHONE	252-636-5553 | 800-849-5553 | Fax 252-636-5553
CONTACT	info@aeriebedandbreakfast.com | www.aeriebedandbreakfast.com
FEATURES	9 Rooms; Private baths | Children age 2 and older welcome | No pets, resident dog | Will accommodate guests' special dietary needs

The historical Street-Ward residence, circa 1882, is home to New Bern's premiere B&B, guest house and conference center. The Aerie B&B features nine well-appointed rooms each with a private bath, modern amenities, and tasteful décor that reflects the home's late Victorian heritage. The Aerie is one block from Tryon Palace, the colonial governor's mansion for North Carolina, and within walking distance to historic downtown New Bern, home of fine dining, antique shops, marinas, and the birthplace of Pepsi.

Hepburn & Tracy Peach/Raspberry Bake

Yield: 14 servings

"We call this Hepburn and Tracy on our menu because it's both sweet and tart! Everyone loves it and requests the recipe."—Innkeeper

Filling

3 large cans peaches
¾ cup defrosted raspberries, mixed with 2 Tbsp sugar

Drain peaches, place into 9x13-inch baking dish and cut peaches into small pieces. Mix in the raspberry sauce.

Biscuit Topping

2¼ cups all-purpose flour   3 Tbsp sugar
3 Tbsp sugar   1 Tbsp milk
1½ tsp baking powder
¼ tsp salt
¼ tsp soda
8 Tbsp chilled butter, cut into small pieces
1½ cups sour cream

Preheat oven to 350°F. In a bowl, place all the dry ingredients together—cut the butter into it—making meal-like crumbs. Add the sour cream and mix until dough is all wet. Take a small scoop and make little balls and place on top of the peaches. Each serving gets two balls. The 9x13-inch baking dish will get 14 servings—4 balls across and 7 balls down. Mix the sugar and the milk together and brush on the balls. Bake for approximately 45–50 minutes. After baking, place on top of stove and cover with aluminum foil to keep warm.

To serve, place one ball upside down in a compote glass, spoon some of the peaches and raspberries on top and then add the other ball. Top with a little whipped cream and a sprig of mint.

Andon-Reid Inn B&B

INNKEEPER Rachel Reid

ADDRESS 92 Daisy Avenue, Waynesville, NC 28786

TELEPHONE 828-452-3089 | 800-293-6190

CONTACT info@andonreidinn.com | www.andonreidinn.com

FEATURES 5 Rooms; Private baths | No pets | Motorcycle friendly including garage space

This turn-of-the-century home, built in 1902, reflects all the beauty, grace, and charm that could be manifested in this traditional style of architecture. Large windows, tall ceilings, extensive oak hardwood floors, and veranda porches that wrap around the house are but a few of the original attributes beckoning for you to enjoy our complimentary mountain views.

Our guestrooms are large, comfortable, and have well-appointed furnishings to complement their surroundings. Each room offers a private bath, fireplace, glorious views, and many distinctive features that will contribute to your comfort, relaxation, and romance. Plenty of off-street parking for all of our guests—no hassle parking. We're less than one mile from the downtown center of Waynesville and minutes from Maggie Valley, Cherokee, and Asheville. Walk into town for shopping, dining, and the many Waynesville attractions—the scenery is breathtaking. The Andon-Reid Inn B&B is at the foothills of the Great Smoky Mountains, the Blue Ridge Parkway, and the Pisgah National Forest.

Mexican Frittata

Yield: 6 servings

½ cup salsa
¼ cup grated Parmesan cheese
¼ cup green pepper
¼ cup asparagus
¼ cup broccoli
½ cup onions
½ cup mushrooms
¼ cup artichokes
½ cup ham
½ cup sausage
 1 glove garlic
½ cup cup cheddar cheese
 8 eggs

Preheat oven to 350°F. Pour salsa over bottom of a 9-inch pie plate. Sprinkle shredded Parmesan cheese over salsa. Sauté the veggies and meat and spread half of veggies/meat over Parmesan cheese. Sprinkle cheddar cheese over veggies and put the rest of veggies over cheese. Beat 8 eggs and pour over veggies. Bake for 35–40 minutes.

AppleWood Manor Inn B&B

INNKEEPERS	Larry & Nancy Merrill
ADDRESS	62 Cumberland Circle, Asheville, NC 28801
TELEPHONE	828-254-2244	800-442-2197	Fax 828-254-0899
CONTACT	innkeeper@applewoodmanor.com	www.applewoodmanor.com
FEATURES	5 Rooms; 1 Cottage; Private baths	Children age 12 and older welcome	Pets permitted in the Cortland Cottage only, 2 resident Silky Terriers	Will accommodate guests' special dietary needs	Wireless Internet

Located in the historic Montford District of Ashevillle, AppleWood Manor Inn sits on a quiet acre and a half of "country in the city" surrounded by giant oaks, pines, maples, and a variety of flora. The manor is just 3 miles from the breathtaking Biltmore Estate, a short 10-minute drive to the Blue Ridge Parkway, and a 25-minute stroll past magnificent old homes to downtown Asheville. In a time when so much is overlooked in the hustle-bustle of daily life, we invite you to romance yourselves with a stay at our lovely B&B to discover a person-alized pampering experience unlike any other.

All of our accommodations are garnished with fresh flowers and feature king or queen-size beds with fine linens, beautiful antiques, private en-suite baths, television with built-in DVD players and iPod or iHome clock radios. Some guestrooms include fireplaces, private balconies, ceiling fans, and more.

Chocolate Banana Walnut Bread

Yield: 12 servings

"This is one of our guest's favorite breads. I had to come up with something to use up my ripe bananas and was bored with plain banana bread. This is thickly sliced, toasted and served with cream cheese on the side."—Innkeeper

2 eggs	1 cup sugar
1¼ cups mashed over-ripe bananas	2 tsp baking powder
½ cup canola oil	4 oz. each semi sweet and milk chocolate bars, coarsely chopped
¼ cup milk	
2 cups all-purpose flour	½ cup hand-chopped walnuts
⅛ tsp salt	

Preheat oven to 350°F. In a bowl, stir eggs, bananas, oil, and milk until well blended. In a separate bowl, combine flour, salt, sugar and baking powder; stir until blended. Add egg mixture to dry mixture, folding in a little. Add chocolate and walnuts; do not over mix. Spray a 9x5-inch loaf pan with canola oil. Pour banana mixture into loaf pan. Bake 1 hour and 7 minutes or until cake tester inserted in thickest part of bread comes out clean. Remove from oven and allow pan to come to room temperature. Hold pan upside down over plastic wrap to remove bread from pan. Use two separate sheets of plastic wrap to seal. Freeze or allow to setup in refrigerator for a minimum of 48 hours.

To serve, slice and broil until toasted. This can last in the refrigerator for a week if double plastic wrapped.

ARROWHEAD INN

INNKEEPERS	Gloria & Phil Tebeo
ADDRESS	106 Mason Road, Durham, NC 27712
TELEPHONE	800-528-2207
CONTACT	info@arrowheadinn.com	www.arrowheadinn.com
FEATURES	4 Rooms; 3 Suites; 2 Cottages; Private baths	Children welcome	No pets	Handicap accessible	Will accommodate guests' special dietary needs

The Arrowhead Inn is the only AAA Four Diamond and Select Registry B&B in the Triangle area of Raleigh, Durham, and Chapel Hill. The inn has been featured in *Southern Living, House and Garden, Food & Wine, USA Today,* and *Old House Journal.*

Awake to an abundant feast with such treats as puffed pancakes, blueberry French toast, fresh herb frittatas, yeast breads, and baked fruits. Enjoy rich coffee and the sounds of Bach while engaged in quiet conversation.

Ginger Scones

Yield: 12 Scones

3 cups all-purpose flour

⅓ cup sugar

1 Tbsp plus 1 tsp baking powder

¼ tsp grated lemon zest

1 stick plus 3 Tbsp unsalted butter, chilled and diced

¾ cup plus 2 Tbsp whipping cream or buttermilk, divided

⅔ cup diced crystallized (candied) ginger

Preheat oven to 400°F. In a food processor, combine flour, sugar, baking powder, and lemon zest. Add butter and pulse until mixture resembles a coarse meal (or cut in butter by hand with 2 knives). Transfer flour mixture to a large bowl and make a well in center. Add ¾ cup of cream to well and stir with a fork just until flour mixture is moistened. Stir in ginger.

Transfer dough to a floured surface and knead gently until smooth, about 8 turns. Divide dough in half and pat each portion into a ¾-inch-thick round. Cut each round into 6 wedges and place on a lightly buttered baking sheet, spacing scones 1-inch apart. Brush tops with the remaining 2 tablespoons of cream. Bake for about 18 minutes, until light brown. Cool completely, then store in an airtight container at room temperature.

Note: These scones can be baked 1 day ahead. Simply rewarm them in a preheated 350°F oven before serving.

At Cumberland Falls Bed and Breakfast Inn

INNKEEPERS	Patti & Gary Wiles
ADDRESS	254 Cumberland Avenue, Asheville, NC 28801
TELEPHONE	888-743-2557
CONTACT	fallsinn@aol.com | www.cumberlandfalls.com
FEATURES	5 Rooms; Private baths | Children age 12 and older welcome | No pets | Handicap accessibility possible | Will accommodate guests' special dietary needs

At Cumberland Falls Bed and Breakfast Inn is casual and elegant. Feel the richness of the original quilted maple woodwork that adorns the foyer. The living room has bay windows and ten-foot ceilings—you could describe this room as eclectic, from the camel leather sofa to the tapestry high-back chairs. Pick a book off the shelf and take a seat by the original wood-burning fireplace or enjoy the view of the gardens from the unique sunroom.

At Cumberland Falls Bed and Breakfast Inn is located in the historic Montford District, three miles from the Biltmore Estate and close to all that Asheville has to offer.

Eggs Piquant Florentine

Yield: 6 servings

²/₃ cup mayonnaise

Dash salt

⅛ tsp pepper

1 tsp Worcestershire sauce

½ tsp onion

¼ cup milk

1 cup sharp New York Cheddar grated

1 bag baby spinach washed and dried

6 eggs

Preheat oven to 350°F. Butter six custard cups or ramekins. In a sauce-pan combine the mayonnaise, salt, pepper, Worcestershire sauce, and onion. Add the milk, gradually blending until smooth. Add the cheese and cook over low heat, stirring constantly for about 5 minutes until thick and smooth. Place a small amount of the sauce in the bottom of the custard cup or ramekin. Cover with about 3 tablespoons of spinach and break an egg (or two, if you would prefer) into the cup or ramekin. Cover up the egg with 2 tablespoons of the sauce and if you use two eggs maybe a little more. Add a little sprinkle of the remainder of the grated cheese if you would like, or some bread crumbs are nice as an alternative.

Place in oven and bake for about 12 minutes. Test the yolk on the egg by touch and serve either softened or a bit harder.

BEAUFORT HOUSE INN

INNKEEPERS	Christina & Jim Muth
ADDRESS	61 North Liberty Street, Asheville, NC 28801
TELEPHONE	828-254-8334	800-261-2221
CONTACT	innkeeper@beauforthouse.com	www.beauforthouse.com
FEATURES	6 Main house rooms; 2 Terrace rooms with private entrance; 3 Cottages; Private baths	Children over 12 years of age welcome	No pets

Enjoy the warmth and friendly atmosphere of this one-of-a-kind historic property. Built in 1894, this historic home has been meticulously restored as a romantic B&B, with an air of casual luxury and elegance—the perfect environment for an exceptional getaway experience. Listed on the National Register of Historic Places, this beautiful Queen Anne Victorian is situated on 1.5 acres in the quiet, residential Chestnut Historic District. It provides an oasis of beautifully landscaped grounds, gardens, and waterfalls just a half-mile stroll from the vibrant activities of downtown Asheville.

We think you will find that the casual setting and warm ambiance of the Inn is enhanced by our 11 guestrooms, each of which offers unique amenities—private baths, two-person Jacuzzis, gas log-burning fireplaces, king- and queen-size beds, luxury linens, LCD TVs, DVD library, WiFi throughout the Inn and much, much more.

Asparagus Spinach Cheese Quiche

Yield: 6 servings

¾ cup (roughly) blanched fresh asparagus
8 eggs, organic are best
¾ cup whipping cream or half & half cream
1 pastry round
   dry basil
¼ cup shredded hard Parmesan cheese, not grated
¼ cup fresh baby spinach, enough to cover one layer of pie surface
½ cup aged shredded cheddar cheese

Preheat oven to 400°F. Cut asparagus on angle and blanch in boiling water until just bright green, set aside. Blend eggs and cream with mixer until well combined. Line pie plate with pastry round and sprinkle with ample amount of dry basil. Layer Parmesan cheese, spinach, aged cheddar cheese, and lastly, chopped asparagus. Cover with egg/cream mixture. Bake at 400°F for first 15 minutes of baking, then reduce to 375°F for last 30 minutes of baking time or until set in middle.

Tip: If pastry or top of quiche are getting too browned before quiche is completely "set" in the middle, just lay a sheet of tinfoil gently over the top … this will prevent further browning.

Benjamin W. Best House

INNKEEPERS	Ossie & Mary Betty Kearney
ADDRESS	2029 Mewborn Church Road, Snow Hill, NC 28580
TELEPHONE	252-747-5054	866-633-0229	Fax 252-747-8327
CONTACT	benjaminwbest@embarqmail.com	www.bwbestinn.com
FEATURES	1 Room, 1 Cottage; Private baths

This National Registry Historic Property (circa 1845–50) is situated in rural Greene County on a working farm, conveniently located among the cities of Goldsboro, Wilson, Kinston, and Greenville, making this area the "hub" of eastern North Carolina.

This pre-Civil War Greek Revival structure, with large expansive rooms, offers simple pleasures with charming country living while enjoying modern conveniences. Guests may choose their pace in life by walking the grounds to the fishpond nearby or stopping to watch our herds in the pasture as they graze. Eco-tourism and agri-tourism enthusiasts can contact us for special local activities including tours, local flavors, historical sites, and kayaking the Contentnea. Wedding couples may choose the grand front portico for a quaint country wedding ceremony and reception to follow on the expansive grounds.

Chocolate Breakfast Muffins

Yield: 18 muffins

²/₃ cup cocoa
1¾ cups unbleached all-purpose flour
1¼ cups light brown sugar
1 tsp baking powder
1 tsp baking soda
¾ tsp salt
1 cup chocolate chips
2 large eggs
1 cup milk
2 tsp vanilla extract
1 stick melted butter

Preheat oven to 400°F. In a bowl, whisk together the cocoa, flour, brown sugar, baking powder, baking soda, salt and chocolate chips. Set aside. In a separate bowl, whisk together the eggs, milk, and vanilla. Add wet ingredients along with melted butter to dry ingredients, stirring to blend. Scoop batter into muffin cups (paper cups or greased), place in oven and bake for 14 minutes.

Big Mill B&B

INNKEEPER Chloe G.Tuttle

ADDRESS 1607 Big Mill Road, Williamston, NC 27892

TELEPHONE 252-792-8787

CONTACT info@bigmill.com | www.bigmill.com

FEATURES 5 Rooms; 2 Suites; Private baths | Children age 10 and older welcome (Call for younger children) | No pets, resident cat (Moses) | Will accommodate guests' special dietary needs

"My folks moved into this house in 1922 … I was born here and it is still a family farm."—Innkeeper

The Big Mill B&B sits amid acres of farmland and forest in the quiet coastal plain of eastern North Carolina, about two hours from Raleigh and Norfolk, in a lush landscape where streams and rivers meander through cypress swamps and fertile farmland.

With over 200 acres of grounds, you can walk in the landscaped gardens, wander through woodlands, or explore the original farm outbuildings. Shaded by stately, 95-year-old pecan trees planted by the owner's parents, the house has been in the innkeeper's family since 1922.

Almond, Honey and Oat Granola

Yield: 11 or 12 one-cup servings

"The only way I can get my plumber to come in a hurry is to promise his assistant some of my granola!"—Innkeeper

6 cups old fashioned whole grain rolled oats (not quick-cooking)
2 cups whole, raw almonds, with skins
1 cup raw pumpkin seeds
1 cup raw sunflower seeds (unsalted)
1 cup firmly packed brown sugar
½ cup honey, heated
⅓ cup vegetable, corn, or canola oil
⅛ tsp salt
1 tsp vanilla

Preheat oven to 350°F. Seriously grease a heavy 12x17-inch cookie sheet with a lip. In a large bowl, stir together the oats, almonds, pumpkin seeds, sunflower seeds, and brown sugar; break up any brown sugar lumps.

Heat the honey, either in a microwave for 1–2 minutes or in a small saucepan on the stove. In a medium-size bowl, combine the honey, oil, vanilla and salt. Add the honey mixture to the dry mixture and stir until well mixed.

Spread the granola mixture on the greased cookie sheet. Mixture will be fairly thick. Pay attention! This granola will burn easily. (I was once in the barn out back and blackened a pan of granola, setting off the alarm and really stinking up the Bed and Breakfast. Guests decided they might not like this black granola!)

Bake for 15 minutes. Stir the granola. Cook for 8 minutes more, stir again. Continue cooking and stirring until granola is golden in color. Remove from oven–remember that granola will continue to cook after you remove it from the oven. Stir again, cool and store in air-tight container.

BILTMORE VILLAGE INN

INNKEEPER	Aaron Hazelton
ADDRESS	119 Dodge Street, Asheville, NC 28803
TELEPHONE	828-274-8707
CONTACT	info@biltmorevillageinn.com | www.biltmorevillageinn.com
FEATURES	7 Guest rooms; Private baths | Children age 10 and over welcome | 2 Pet-friendly rooms | Wireless Internet | Gourmet 3-course breakfast | Complimentary wine/cheese tasting each afternoon

The closest of Asheville's B&B inns to the Biltmore Estate, the Biltmore Village Inn is located on top of Reed Hill, above Biltmore Village. The entrance to the Biltmore Estate can be seen from the inn's tower sitting area.

From the tower and the porch, you can see why Samuel Reed, George Vanderbilt's lawyer, situated his house here after he sold Asheville's first multi-millionaire the property for Biltmore Village. It commands a 360-degree view of the mountains and overlooks the village and the Swannanoa River Valley below.

Raspberry Orange Croissants

Yield: 6 servings

- 6 medium croissants, halved lengthwise
- 1 (8-oz.) pkg. cream cheese, softened
- 1 cup fresh or frozen raspberries (thawed)
- 8 eggs
- ½ cup sugar
- 1 cup half & half
- 1 tsp nutmeg
- 1 tsp almond extract
- ½ cup orange marmalade
- ¼ cup orange juice

Plan ahead, this dish needs to be started the night before.

Grease or lightly oil a 7x11-inch or 9x13-inch baking dish. Spread the 12 croissant halves with cream cheese. Arrange some raspberries on top of each croissant bottom, then sandwich with croissant tops. Place croissants in baking dish. In a medium bowl, beat eggs. Add sugar, half & half, nutmeg, and almond extract; mix well and pour over croissants. In a small bowl, mix marmalade and orange juice; spoon over croissants. Cover and refrigerate overnight.

The next morning, preheat oven to 350°F. Bake croissants for about 40 minutes, until custard is puffy and slightly browned. Cut apart to serve.

Blooming Garden Inn

INNKEEPERS	Frank and Dolly Pokrass
ADDRESS	513 Holloway Street, Durham, NC 27701
TELEPHONE	919-687-0801
CONTACT	bloominggardeninn@msn.com | www.bloominggardeninn.com
FEATURES	4 rooms, including two Jacuzzi suites featuring oversize Jacuzzis and lots of extras; Private baths | Supervised children welcome | No pets | Will accommodate guests' special dietary needs, with notice | Gated | Wi-Fi

"The work and love you have put into restoring the house and opening it to guests from around the world are an inspiration."—Guest

The house was built by James N. Umstead around 1890 in the Queen Anne style. The Durham B&B features a huge wrap-around porch with 21 Tuscan columns. Dolly and Frank spent nearly

three years in intensive restoration of the property and opened for business in the fall of 1990. High curved ceilings, heart-pine wainscotting, raised wood panels, nine original mantels, doors (put together with pegs) with original hardware, and all-original southern pine flooring will delight the historical buff. Antiques of the period are abundantly distributed throughout.

The yard is fully enclosed with custom front fencing and gate. Mature floral gardens and flowering trees highlight the landscaping. The back yard is suitable for private events. There are four primary guest rooms, each with its own private bath. Each has its own distinctive character and is highlighted by antiques of the period. For the convenience of our guests we are open year-round, including major holidays.

Crêpes

Yield: about a dozen crêpes, depending on size.

Ingredients:
- 2 large eggs
- 1 Tbsp canola oil
- 1 tsp honey
- 1¼ cups whole milk (or soy)
- ¾ cup unbleached flour
- ½ cup chopped walnuts
- dash salt

Filling:
- 1 (8-oz. pkg.) cream cheese
- 4 oz. ricotta cheese
- 2 oz. sour cream
- 1 Tbsp sugar
- lemon zest
- (mix filling ingredients in separate bowl with fork; sweeten to taste)

Topping:
6 oz. fresh raspberries or chopped strawberries in small bowl with several teaspoons of fresh orange juice

In a blender mix the above ingredients in the order given. Use a narrow spatula to clean down sides and re-mix briefly. Transfer mixture to a large measuring cup for easy pouring. Pour a small amount of mixture to test onto hot 9-inch crêpe pan (lightly coated with the oil); if it sizzles, it's ready. Remove sample and pour just enough batter to cover the bottom of the pan. Cook just long enough to see the browning of the edges. Carefully flip the crêpe over for about ten seconds and remove to a stacking plate.

On a large plate, lay one of the crêpes (inside up) and apply several spoonfuls of filling across crêpe near one end. Carefully roll crêpe around filling and put aside. Repeat for as many crêpes as you intend to serve. Keep prepared crêpes warm in oven or under cover. When just about ready to serve, place on serving plate, apply warmed topping mixture with a spoon, and (optional) garnish with a dollop of whipped cream. Garnish plate with twisted orange slice and/or sprig of parsley.

Brookside Mountain Mist Inn B&B

INNKEEPERS	Carolyn Gendreau and Dina Giunta
ADDRESS	142 Country Club Drive, Waynesville, NC 28786
TELEPHONE	828-452-6880 | 1-877-452-6880
CONTACT	info@brooksidemountainmistbb.com | www.brooksidemountainmistbb.com
FEATURES	5 Rooms; Private baths | Children age 12 and over welcome | No pets | Biker friendly with garage parking for up to 10 motorcycles | Wireless Internet

At Brookside Mountain Mist Inn you'll find luxury accommodations with oversized immaculate guestrooms, three-course gourmet breakfasts, privacy, a quiet park-like setting with beautiful mountain views, and a convenient location near the Great Smoky Mountains, Asheville, Biltmore Estate, with plenty of things to do. Enjoy views of the Blue Ridge Mountains from our terrace. Browse the downtown Waynesville shops and galleries. Savor a variety of cuisine in many nearby restaurants. Play golf next door. Drive the Blue Ridge Parkway, just four miles away. Hike, bike, raft, kayak, and fish with lofty mountains (including legendary Cold Mountain), waterfalls, and scenic rivers.

After exploring our area, relax peacefully at our quiet oasis with five spacious, tastefully decorated rooms, each with private bath, fireplace, sitting area, and cable TV. Guestrooms are beautifully furnished and include the "little extras" to be expected at a luxury inn or hotel such as soft robes, hair dryers, iron, and bath amenities.

Cinnamon Chip Scones

Yield: 10–12 scones

"The cinnamon chips are hard to find in local stores so you may have to order them online. Sorry, they won't ship them during the warmer months because you tend to get a gooey mess upon arrival!"—Innkeeper

- 2 cups flour
- 2 tsp baking powder
- ½ tsp baking soda
- ½ tsp salt
- 2 Tbsp sugar
- ½ cup butter
- 1 cup cinnamon baking chips
- 1 egg, separated
- 1 tsp vanilla
- ¾ cup buttermilk
- cinnamon sugar

Preheat oven to 375°F. Combine flour, baking powder, baking soda, salt and sugar in mixing bowl. Cut in the butter. Stir in the cinnamon chips. In a separate bowl, combine egg yolk, vanilla, and buttermilk. Add to dry ingredients, mixing completely by hand. On a floured surface roll out dough by hand into ½-inch thickness. Cut into scones with 3-inch cookie cutter and place on ungreased cookie sheet. Brush egg white over scones and sprinkle cinnamon sugar over scones. Bake 18–22 minutes. Cool scones a couple of minutes before serving.

Buffalo Tavern B&B

INNKEEPER	Doc Adams
ADDRESS	958 W. Buffalo Road, West Jefferson, NC 28694
TELEPHONE	336-877-9080 | 1-877-615-9678
CONTACT	buffalotavernbnb@aol.com | www.buffalotavern.com
FEATURES	3 Rooms; One suite; Private baths | Children over age 12 welcome with at least one parent | No pets | Wireless high speed Internet

Historic Buffalo Tavern B&B is located in the North Carolina Blue Ridge Mountains near West Jefferson, Lansing, Todd, Glendale Springs, Jefferson, Blowing Rock, and Boone, in Ashe County. Enjoy a private mountain getaway in a relaxing country setting that is only a short drive to downtown West Jefferson Arts District, area attractions including historic Todd and Glendale Springs, and a scenic 40-minute drive to Boone and Blowing Rock.

All three guestrooms feature a private bath with shower, queen-size bed dressed with soft cotton sheets, a cozy down comforter, and four wonderfully inviting pillows, an electric fireplace and a compact disc player. Satellite television is available. All rooms have a two-person antique claw foot soaking tub and beautiful wooden floors from the days when the Tavern was built. The President's Suite is a wonderfully inviting three-room area with the second room that has a wet bar with sink, fridge, microwave, dishes, glasses, sitting area, and closet.

Herb-Baked Eggs

Yield: 8 servings

"These are individual ramekin bakes. I use 5x5-inch ramekins. It is simple and a delicious way to serve eggs!"—Innkeeper

3	Tbsp basil, dried or fresh
3	Tbsp thyme, dried or fresh
8	tomato slices (or small ham slices)
2	cups shredded mild cheddar cheese
24	whole eggs
8	heaping Tbsp fat-free sour cream
1	tsp dry mustard (or to taste)
½	tsp nutmeg (or to taste)

Balsamic Glaze:
balsamic vinegar
sugar

Preheat oven to 375°F. Spray each ramekin with nonstick cooking spray. Spread ¼ tsp each of basil and thyme in the bottom of each ramekin. Lay down one slice of tomato. Divide the shredded cheddar cheese between the 8 ramekins and place on top of the tomato. In a large mixing bowl, add all 24 eggs, 8 heaping Tbsp of fat-free sour cream, the dry mustard and nutmeg. Whip thoroughly. Pour the egg mixture over the cheddar cheese in each ramekin. Bake for 35–45 minutes or until a toothpick comes out clean.

Immediately upon taking the ramekins out of the oven, drizzle about 1 Tbsp of balsamic glaze* on top of each and serve piping hot with fruit and a baked good!

*Balsamic glaze is ½ bottle of balsamic vinegar and 3 Tbsp of sugar. Bring the vinegar and sugar to a boil and remove from stove to reduce. Save in a bottle in the fridge until needed again.

CAROLINA B&B

INNKEEPERS James and Susan Murray

ADDRESS 177 Cumberland Avenue, Asheville NC 28801

TELEPHONE 828-254-3608 | 888-254-3608 | Fax 828-254-3608

CONTACT info@carolinabb.com | www.carolinabb.com

FEATURES 5 Suites; 1 Cottage; Private baths | Children age 10 and older welcome | No pets | Will accommodate guests' special dietary needs | Wireless Internet

Built in 1901 by one of the architects working on the Biltmore Estate, this gracious Arts & Crafts style home has seen history unfold. It became a boarding house in the 1930s and it was then that David Webb, world famous designer of jewelry for Jackie Kennedy, Doris Day, and Gwen Stefani among others, lived and worked in the small cottage on the property. James and Susan bought the property in 2009 and have filled it with beautiful art and antiques from their 27 years of living in Europe and Asia. The comfortable elegance of the furnishings, acclaimed home cooking, and close proximity of downtown Asheville have made it the Inn of choice for many visitors.

Murray Cookies

Yield: 2 dozen cookies

Cream together:

¾ cup vegetable shortening

1 cup packed brown sugar

½ cup sugar

1 egg

¼ cup water

1 tsp vanilla

Mix together and add to creamed mixture:

2½ cups oatmeal

1½ cups flour

1 tsp baking soda

½ tsp salt

Stir in

½ bag chocolate chips

½ bag butterscotch chips

Bake on greased cookie sheets 12–15 minutes at 350°F. Wait one minute and remove from oven.

Carol's Garden Inn

INNKEEPERS	**Carol & Steve Barden**
ADDRESS	**2412 S. Alston Avenue, Durham, NC 27713**
TELEPHONE	**919-680-6777	1-877-922-6777**
CONTACT	**carol@carolsgardeninn.com	www.carolsgardeninn.com	**
	www.WeddingsAtCarolsGardenInn.com
FEATURES	**3 Rooms; Private baths	Well-behaved children welcome	No pets, but we**
	can arrange boarding nearby

This circa 1910 home has been completely renovated to take you back to a bygone era of Southern hospitality. You can relax on the deck and watch the colorful fish in the water garden, sit by the large lower pond, stroll the grounds, or restore your soul in your beautifully decorated, spacious, quiet bedroom with private bath and whirlpool tub. In the morning, enjoy a great breakfast to start your day. The Inn is also a great place for a wedding, large or small.

Peach Pecan Upside-Down Pancake

Yield: 6 servings

- 2 Tbsp butter, melted
- 2 Tbsp packed light brown sugar
- 1 Tbsp maple syrup
- ¼ cup peach Schnapps liqueur
- 2 or 3 Tbsp pecan pieces
- ½ pkg. (1 lb.) frozen unsweetened peach slices, thawed
- 2 eggs
- ½ cup milk
- ½ tsp vanilla
- ⅔ cup biscuit baking mix

Preheat oven to 400°F. Spray 8- or 9-inch pie pan with nonstick cooking spray. Pour butter into pie pan. Sprinkle on brown sugar and maple syrup. Add peach Schnapps liqueur. Sprinkle with pecans. Place peach slices in single layer on top in a decorative circle.

Whisk together eggs, milk and vanilla in medium bowl. Stir in biscuit baking mix until just combined. Pour batter over peaches. Bake 15 to 18 minutes until lightly browned and firm to the touch. Remove from oven. Let cool 1 minute. Run knife around outer edge.

Invert pancake over serving plate. Slice into 6 servings. Serve with additional syrup if desired.

Chalet Inn

INNKEEPERS	George & Hanneke Ware
ADDRESS	285 Lone Oak Drive, Dillsboro, NC 28725
TELEPHONE	828-586-0251 | 800-789-8024
CONTACT	ParadiseFound@ChaletInn.com | www.chaletinn.com
FEATURES	4 Rooms; 7 Suites; Private baths | Children age 12 and older welcome | No pets | Will accommodate guests' special dietary needs

The Chalet Inn is the closest B&B and boutique hotel to the main entrance of the Great Smoky Mountains National Park. AAA 3-Diamond lodging, the Chalet Inn includes two buildings constructed in traditional Alpine style, nestled in a 22-acre private forest where the Smoky Mountains meet the Blue Ridge Mountains in western North Carolina.

Chalet Inn's Apfelkuchen (Apple Cake)

Yield: 8 servings

11 oz. plain flour
8 oz. sugar, divided
5 oz. butter
2 egg yolks
1 pinch salt
1 lb. cooking apples (or drained, canned apples)
1 lemon, juiced
1 pinch cinnamon
2 oz. raisins
2 oz. ground hazelnuts
2 oz. ground almonds
2 Tbsp apricot jam
2 oz. icing sugar
2 Tbsp Kirsch or cherry brandy

Sift the flour into a bowl. Stir in 5 ounces of the sugar and rub in the butter. Add egg yolks and salt, and mix quickly to a dough. Chill for 20 minutes.

Preheat oven to 400°F. Roll out half the dough to line a 10-inch flan ring. Bake for 15 minutes.

Peel, core and slice the apples and mix with remaining sugar, lemon juice, cinnamon, raisins and nuts. Moisten with a little water to blend. Spoon filling into the baked pastry shell and smooth out. Roll out the remaining dough to cover the filling (you can also make decorative strips to cover the flan). Bake in the preheated oven for 30 minutes. Cool in the pan overnight.

Warm the jam and spread over the cake. Combine the icing sugar and Kirsch, spread over the jam and leave to set.

THE COVE B&B

INNKEEPERS	Erin and Chad O'Neal
ADDRESS	21 Loop Road, Ocracoke, NC 27960 | PO Box 1300, Ocracoke, NC 27960
TELEPHONE	252-928-4192 | Fax 252-928-4092
CONTACT	info@thecovebb.com | www.thecovebb.com
FEATURES	4 Rooms; 3 Suites; Private baths | Children age 15 and older welcome | No pets | Will accommodate guests' special dietary needs if notified in advance

Welcome to beautiful Ocracoke, on the Outer Banks. After a relaxing ferry ride, the Cove B&B provides a quiet location for a great getaway. Start the day with a scrumptious breakfast, take one of the Inn's bikes and spend hours exploring Ocracoke's seashore (ranked third on Dr. Beach's "America's Best Beaches 2004") and the village, paddle around in a kayak, go charter fishing in the Gulfstream, or simply do nothing.

Stretch out and unwind. The inn's tastefully decorated rooms and suites offer a special setting for honeymoons, anniversaries, or just a weekend away. All guest rooms have a queen-size bed, private furnished balcony, central AC, hair dryer, ceiling fan, DVD player, and satellite TV.

Pineapple Breakfast Dessert

Yield: 6 to 8 servings

"When we serve our pineapple breakfast dessert, our guests pass on extra biscuits to leave room for more pineapple!" —Innkeeper

2 (20-oz.) cans pineapple (tidbits, crushed or chunks), drained
1 cup grated extra-sharp cheddar cheese
1 cup sugar
¼ cup all-purpose flour
1 sleeve Ritz crackers, crushed
1 stick butter, melted

Preheat oven to 350°F. Grease a 9x13-inch baking dish. Combine pineapple, cheese, sugar and flour; spread in the baking dish. Combine crackers and butter; sprinkle over pineapple mixture. Bake for 30 minutes. Serve warm.

Cheddar cheese originated in the village of Cheddar in the Somerset region of England. It's a firm, cow's-milk cheese that ranges in flavor from mild to sharp, and in color from natural white to pumpkin orange. Orange cheddars are colored with a natural dye called annatto.

CULPEPPER INN

INNKEEPER   Holly Koerber

ADDRESS   609 West Main Street, Elizabeth City, NC 27909

TELEPHONE   252-335-9235

CONTACT   innkeeper@culpepperinn.com | www.culpepperinn.com

FEATURES   11 Rooms (including 1 suite); Private baths | No pets | ADA compliant room for those with special needs

Tucked away in historic, beautiful downtown Elizabeth City, the Culpepper Inn is just a one-hour drive from Norfolk International Airport, Virginia Beach oceanfront, and the Outer Banks resort areas of eastern North Carolina. This 1935 three-story brick Georgian Revival style manor is situated in the center of the historic district of Elizabeth City. The Inn is only six blocks from the center of town and the harbor front on the Pasquotank River.

The Inn features eleven guest rooms, four in the Main House, one suite in the Carriage House, and six in the Camellia Guest House. The Inn is surrounded by lush grounds with beautiful old live oak and magnolia trees, and

Culpepper Inn Bed and Breakfast

the property is accented by over 20 different camellia trees and bushes. The Tavern Room, in-ground pool, and the rockers on the porch, as well as the fairy garden with a water feature invite our guests to linger and relax during their stay. The Culpepper Inn is available to host family reunions, weddings, meetings, and events inside the Inn with room for up to 75, and outside on the grounds with room for up to 150.

Caramelized Baked French Toast

Yield: 6–8 servings

1	cup dark brown sugar
3	Tbsp Karo syrup
6	Tbsp butter
1	can no-sugar added apple or peach pie filling or canned undrained, blackberries or strawberries
18	slices day-old white bread (may use cinnamon bread too & remove crusts if you prefer)
6	eggs
2	cups milk
1	tsp good quality vanilla
	Freshly grated cinnamon & nutmeg

Plan ahead, this dish needs to be started the night before.

Combine sugar, syrup, and butter in pan, boil for one minute. Pour into greased 9x13-inch dish. Place all the fruit on top of the caramel mixture. Layer bread over mixture. Grate cinnamon and nutmeg over bread (each layer). Mix eggs, milk, and vanilla together and pour over bread until top is moist, do this for 3 layers of bread. You may spread whipped cream cheese on the bread layers before the spices and egg mixture if you like. This is especially good with the strawberry version.

Refrigerate overnight and bake at 350°F degrees for 45 minutes until brown & slightly puffy. Slice and serve. ENJOY!

THE DUKE MANSION

INNKEEPER	The Lynnwood Foundation
ADDRESS	400 Hermitage Road, Charlotte, NC 28207
TELEPHONE	704-714-4400 | 888-202-1009
CONTACT	frontdesk@dukemansion.org | www.dukemansion.org
FEATURES	20 Rooms; Private baths | Children welcome | No pets, resident cats | Handicap accessible | Will accommodate guests' special dietary needs

There is a long tradition of unforgettable hospitality at The Duke Mansion. Today the Inn is dedicated to fine cuisine, remarkable service and beautiful presentation. With an emphasis on Southern charm in the Charlotte tradition, the chefs know how to add just the right flourish to make dining memorable.

Breakfast entrées may include banana pancakes with cranberry butter and maple syrup, eggs Benedict, smoked salmon and spinach quiche, shrimp and grits, or coconut waffles with fruit compote and whipped cream.

Sweet Potato, Artichoke & Crawfish Hash

Yield: 4 servings

½ cup olive oil, divided
½ cup diced onion
¼ cup diced red bell pepper
¼ cup diced yellow bell pepper
¼ cup diced green bell pepper
1 lb. sweet potatoes, diced
1 Tbsp minced garlic
4 oz. cooked crawfish tails, diced
½ cup marinated artichoke heart quarters
¼ cup chopped cilantro
¼ cup chopped parsley
   Salt and black pepper, to taste

Heat ¼ cup of olive oil in a skillet over medium heat. Add onions and red, yellow, and green bell peppers; cook until onions are translucent, then remove from heat and set aside to cool.

Heat remaining ¼ cup of olive oil in a skillet over medium heat. Add sweet potatoes and cook until tender and caramelized. Add bell pepper mixture, garlic, crawfish, artichokes, cilantro, and parsley. Season with salt and pepper. Heat through and serve.

Serve with Pan-Fried North Carolina Brook Trout (see recipe on page 217).

THE FORK

INNKEEPER Debra Graden

ADDRESS 3200 Fork Road, Norwood, NC 28128

TELEPHONE 704-474-4052 ext. 227

CONTACT dgraden@theforkfarm.com | www.forkstables.com

FEATURES 8 Rooms; Private baths | No pets in room —kennels available to board your dog at no charge | Handicap accessible | Wireless Internet

The Fork offers endless activities and adventures to suit a wide range of interests. Not only does The Fork boast world-class equestrian and sporting clays and hunting facilities, but we also provide opportunities for mountain biking, fishing, hiking, and much more; all while surrounded by the pristine beauty of The Fork. Be as active as your heart desires and end the day relaxing in the comforts of our Lodge Bed and Breakfast.

Experience the serene, relaxed atmosphere of the Farm while staying in our gorgeous Lodge with rocking chair porch. Enjoy a delicious continental breakfast in the common kitchen/dining area. The rooms are also connected by a common living area with comfortable seating, a big-screen television, and cozy fireplace.

Nanny's Sticky Buns

Yield: 24 servings

1   pkg. (24) Bridgford Parkerhouse style frozen rolls
2   cups chopped pecans
1   pkg. Jello butterscotch pudding mix (not instant)
½   cup brown sugar
1   tsp cinnamon
1   stick butter

Spray 9x13-inch pan with nonstick cooking spray. Sprinkle with chopped pecans. Arrange frozen rolls on top of pecans. Sprinkle with pudding mix, brown sugar, and cinnamon. Dot with butter. Put in cold oven overnight. Bake at 350°F for 20 minutes. Turn upside down on serving plate. Serve warm.

Brown sugar is white sugar combined with molassas, which gives it a soft texture. All granulated sugar can be stored indefinitely if tightly sealed and kept in a cool, dry place.

Fuquay Mineral Spring Inn

INNKEEPERS	John & Patty Byrne
ADDRESS	333 South Main Street, Fuquay-Varina, NC 27526
TELEPHONE	919-552-3782 | 866-552-3782
CONTACT	jbyrne@fuquayinn.com | www.fuquayinn.com
FEATURES	3 Private Rooms, 1 Carriage House, 1 Suite; Private baths | Children age 12 and older welcome | No Pets | Will accommodate guests' special dietary needs

The Fuquay Mineral Spring Inn & Garden is a Colonial Revival home listed as a local landmark in Wake County. The Inn is located directly across the street from the historic Fuquay Mineral Spring Park and is convenient to Raleigh-Durham, Cary, Fayetteville, and Chapel Hill, as well as such attractions as Exploris, Alltel Pavilion, Raven Rock State Park, the Carolina Hurricanes hockey team and more.

The Inn is perched on a hill overlooking the spring and has a garden with a period gazebo offering great views of the town of Fuquay-Varina.

Hot Jalapeño Crab Dip

Yield: 4 to 6 servings

 1 lb. lump crabmeat
 1 tsp minced garlic
 ½ cup chopped pickled jalapeños (from a jar)
 1 cup grated pepper Jack cheese
 1 tsp Worcestershire sauce
 1 Tbsp hot sauce
 ¼ tsp salt
 ½ cup mayonnaise
 3 oz. Parmigiano-Reggiano cheese, grated
    Crusty bread, for serving

Preheat oven to 350°F. In a medium bowl, combine crab, garlic, jalapeños, pepper Jack cheese, Worcestershire, hot sauce, salt, and mayonnaise; toss gently to mix (take care not to break up lumps of crab). Spoon crab mixture into a shallow, medium baking dish. Sprinkle with Parmigiano-Reggiano cheese. Bake for about 25 minutes, until golden brown. Remove from oven and let stand for 5 minutes. Serve with crusty bread.

GLADE VALLEY B&B

INNKEEPERS	Margaret & Jim Connor
ADDRESS	330 Shaw Lane, Glade Valley, NC 28627
TELEPHONE	336-657-8811 | 800-538-3508
CONTACT	contact@gladevalley.com | www.gladevalley.com
FEATURES	5 Suites; Private baths | Children age 12 and older welcome | No pets

The Glade Valley B&B is the coziest place to stay in Alleghany County. It is located within walking distance of the Blue Ridge Parkway and is less than 7 miles from Sparta. The Inn is nestled on 29 acres of beautiful mountainside that features tall pines, walking trails, and breathtaking views.

Built in 2006 by owners Jim and Margaret Connor, the Glade Valley B&B is perfect for a tranquil escape. The log exterior boasts a large wraparound porch perfect for relaxing with a mountain view and a  cool breeze. It has 5 guest suites with private baths (3 with Jacuzzi tubs and plush guest robes) with individual balcony entrances and many other amenities. Each room is sure to delight you with its national park décor. Our loft library has many books on the area for your convenience. Accommodations also include a full country breakfast. Everything we serve is made fresh and from scratch.

Cinnamon Buns

Yield: 2 dozen rolls

2	pkgs. dry yeast	
½	cup warm water	
2	cups lukewarm milk, scalded then cooled	
⅓	cup sugar	
⅓	cup vegetable oil	
3	tsp baking powder	
2	tsp salt	
1	egg	
6½ – 7½	cups flour, divided	

Filling:

4	Tbsp soft butter
½	cup sugar
1	Tbsp cinnamon

Glaze:

1	cup powdered sugar
1	Tbsp butter
½	tsp vanilla
1–2	Tbsp milk

Dissolve yeast in warm water in a large mixing bowl. Stir in milk, sugar, oil, baking powder, salt, egg, and 2 cups flour. Beat until smooth. Mix in enough remaining flour to make dough easy to handle. Turn onto floured surface and knead until smooth and elastic. Place in a greased bowl and cover. Let rise in a warm place until doubled, about 1½ hours. Punch down dough. Divide in half. Roll one-half into a rectangle— 12x10 inches. Spread 2 tablespoons of butter and sprinkle with cinnamon sugar. Roll up into a roll and seal edge. Stretch to make the roll even.

Cut roll into slices 1 inch thick. Place slightly apart on a greased baking pan. Wrap pan tightly with aluminum foil. Repeat with other half of dough. To bake immediately do not wrap. Can be refrigerated 12–48 hours. Let rise 30 minutes in a warm place. Bake at 350°F uncovered for about 20–30 minutes until light brown. To make glaze, mix together sugar, butter, vanilla and milk, and spread on rolls while they are still warm.

HERREN HOUSE

INNKEEPERS	Michelle & Phil Briggs
ADDRESS	94 East Street, Waynesville, NC 28786
TELEPHONE	828-452-7837 | 855-696-4117
CONTACT	michelle@herrenhouse.com | www.herrenhouse.com
FEATURES	6 Suites; Private baths | Pets welcome | Will accommodate guests' special dietary needs

Herren House combines Victorian charm with a modern, uncluttered and clean elegance, for residents and visitors needing a break from a more hectic pace. This unique nineteenth-century boarding house has been completely restored and offers all updated conveniences that will make your stay extremely comfortable and refreshing. The two lower-level rooms are available for dogs up to 50 pounds with room for a crate. A large, flat parking lot also welcomes motorcycle enthusiasts, with plenty of storage for bicycles and hiking gear.

Herren House and Bridget's Bistro are open to guests and the public year round. We can accommodate wedding receptions, rehearsal dinners, parties, reunions, and retreats. In the warm months, guests can enjoy the beautiful garden area with its gazebo and patio. As if that isn't idyllic enough, there is a huge old-fashioned wraparound porch, perfect for quiet relaxation. The inn is a few minutes away from the Blue Ridge Parkway, the Great

Smoky Mountains National Park, Maggie Valley, and just 30 minutes to Asheville and the Biltmore Estate.

Strawberry French Toast

Yield: 6 servings

1 large loaf French bread
2 eggs
2 cups half & half
1 tsp cinnamon
1 tsp nutmeg
1 tsp vanilla
1 (8-oz.) tub ricotta cheese
2 Tbsp honey
3 Tbsp powdered sugar, divided
1 lb. sliced strawberries soaked in sugar

Cut bread into 12 slices. In a bowl, whisk the eggs, cream, cinnamon, nutmeg, and vanilla. Dip bread in the egg/cream wash. Cook on grill or skillet. In another bowl, blend the ricotta cheese, honey, and 2 tablespoons of sugar. When cooked, spread on cheese/honey mixture. Place strawberries on top and place second slice of bread at an angle. Dust with powdered sugar and top with whipped cream.

HILL HOUSE B&B

INNKEEPER	David Smith
ADDRESS	120 Hillside Street, Asheville, NC 28801
TELEPHONE	828.232.0345	855.447.0002
CONTACT	info@HillHouseBB.com	www.HillHouseBB.com
FEATURES	7 Rooms; 2 Suites; 1 Cottage; Private baths	Pets welcome (in Cottage with approval)	Will accommodate guests' special dietary needs

Hill House.
It's a place with one foot very much in the present and the other in a past we all cherish.

Rooms that hint both of Grandma Knows and Guitar Nights.

A huge, grassy lawn for play and an Appalachian garden for inspiration.

Breakfasts with French-pressed coffee from Javataza, our signature fresh fruit juices, and eggs, cream, breads, cheeses, and who-knows-what surprises all served with a chef's insights.

Situated in the heart of the romantic, offbeat city of Asheville, the American Shangri-La, in the North Carolina Blue Ridge Mountains.

Wild Rice and Mushroom Frittata

Yield: 6 servings

Wild Rice:

2 cups water
½ cup wild rice

Frittata:

2 Tbsp olive oil
1 lb. mixed mushrooms (portabella, shiitake, cremini, etc.), sliced
½ medium red onion, sliced
1 tsp salt
½ tsp pepper
⅛ tsp nutmeg
1 Tbsp fresh rosemary, minced
8 eggs
2 Tbsp fresh parsley, chopped
¾ cup Parmesan cheese

For the rice, combine water and rice in a small saucepan and bring to a boil. Cover and reduce heat to low. Simmer until rice is tender but with a slight bite, about 40–50 minutes. Drain and set aside.

Preheat oven to 400°F. Heat oil in a large skillet. Add mushrooms, red onion, salt, pepper, nutmeg, and rosemary. Cook until mushrooms release their liquid and the pan is dry. Allow to cool in the pan while preparing the eggs.

Beat the eggs in a large bowl. Add parsley, mushroom mixture, rice, Parmesan cheese, and mix together well. Place mixture in a greased 10-inch ceramic pie pan and bake for 30 minutes or until set.

Home Coming Bed & Breakfast

INNKEEPERS Sam & Deborah Swift

ADDRESS 608 North Bridge Street, Elkin, NC 28621

TELEPHONE 336-526-7772 | Fax 336-835-7776

CONTACT deborah@homecominghouse.com | www.homecominghouse.com

FEATURES 4 Suites; Private baths | No Pets | Will accommodate guests' special dietary needs | Chef Services Available | Wireless Internet | Has maintained a 100 Health Score since opening.

Home ... a love-filled safe and happy haven to rest, relax, and enjoy ... sights and sounds and smells, tastes, and feelings that return you to a place and time when people took time for one another and expressed openly their care and kindness ... where traditions were made and passed forward so the next generations could understand the comforts of grandma's rocking chair ... the joy of music and singing at the piano ... romps in the flower garden ... sunsets from the porch ...

Come and experience the comforts of days gone by where everything is designed to lullaby the body, soul, and mind. Come be our guest ... sample the delights and comforts ... rest, relax, enjoy ... savor the Home Coming experience!

Home ... Where Each Live for the Other and all Live for God.

Red Velvet Cake

Yield: 10 servings

Christmas Cake: The Story of the Red Velvet
Red Cherries commemorate Christ's Drops of Blood Shed on Calvary.
The White Fluffy Icing symbolizes the Purity of Christ. Rich Layers
confirm the Rich goodness of God's Love. The Special Vinegar and
Soda that makes the cake rise commemorates Christ's death on the
Cross as He was given vinegar, and the Soda commemorates the Resur-
rection. The Coconut represents us as sinners becoming clean by our
salvation through the baby Christ Jesus. The Coconut represents us as
sinners becoming clean by our salvation through the baby Christ Jesus.

½ cup shortening or	**Fluffy frosting:**
1 stick butter	1½ cups milk
1½ cups sugar	¾ cup flour
2 eggs	1 box powdered sugar
2 oz. red food coloring	½ cup Crisco shortening
2 level Tbsp cocoa	1 Tbsp vanilla
1 tsp salt	
1 cup buttermilk	1 box coconut
2¼ cups flour	maraschino cherries
1 tsp vanilla	
1 Tbsp vinegar	
1 tsp soda	

Preheat oven to 350°F. In a bowl, cream the butter, sugar, eggs, and
vanilla. Mix in food coloring, cocoa, and salt. Alternately add buttermilk and flour to the cake batter. Mix vinegar and soda in a separate
cup and pour it into the cake batter. Stir until combined. Bake for
30–35 minutes. Let cool. For fluffy frosting, cook milk and flour on
medium high until it thickens. Let cool. Add sugar, Crisco, and vanilla
and beat at high speed until light and fluffy. Frost the cake, sprinkle
heavily with coconut, and top with maraschino cherries.

INN AT BINGHAM SCHOOL

INNKEEPERS	François & Christina Deprez
ADDRESS	NC 54 at Mebane Oaks Road, Chapel Hill, NC 27514
TELEPHONE	919-563-5583 | 800-566-5583
CONTACT	fdeprez@mebtel.net | www.innatbinghamschool.com
FEATURES	4 Rooms; 1 Cottage; Private baths | Children welcome | No pets | Will accommodate guests' special dietary needs | Wireless Internet

The circa 1796 Inn at Bingham School is located just west of Chapel Hill and the University of North Carolina, tucked away on ten acres under large pecan trees. Listed on the National Register of Historic Places, the Inn once served as the homestead for the headmaster of the Bingham School, a preparatory school for young men awaiting entrance to UNC Chapel Hill.

Wake up to an elaborate breakfast served in the dining room or on the patio. Menus are seasonal and may include such specialties as pear almond waffles, baked German pancakes and huevos rancheros. Complimentary wine is served in the evening. Linger by the fire with wine or stroll outside for the French game of Petanque—we have two official courts. Guest rooms are individually decorated with antiques, fine rugs and fabrics—some feature air-jetted bathtubs and fireplaces. Throughout our B&B you'll find plump pillows, fluffy towels, and comfortable reading chairs inviting you to relax and unwind.

Chocolate Chip Cookies

Yield: 3 dozen cookies

2 sticks unsalted butter, room temperature
1 Tbsp glucose
¾ cup brown sugar
¾ cup sugar
2 eggs
1 tsp Madagascar vanilla
1 tsp baking soda
1 tsp salt
2½ cups all-purpose flour
1 (12-oz.) pkg. best quality semi-sweet chocolate chips
   (I prefer Guittard)

Preheat oven to 375°F. In a large bowl, cream together butter, glucose, and sugars. Add eggs one at a time on low speed. Add vanilla, baking soda, salt, and flour. Mix until combined. Stir in chocolate chips. Using 1½-inch scoop, place cookies on a wax paper–lined baking sheet. Freeze for 1 hour or up to 1 month wrapped. Line baking sheet with parchment paper. Place dough 1 inch apart on sheet and bake for 11 minutes. Turn sheet and bake a few more minutes until lightly browned. Cool on cookie sheet for two minutes, then transfer to cooling rack until cooled.

THE INN AT CELEBRITY DAIRY

INNKEEPER	Brit Fleming Pfann
ADDRESS	144 Celebrity Dairy Way, Siler City, NC 27344
TELEPHONE	919-742-5176	877-742-5176
CONTACT	theinn@celebritydairy.com	www.celebritydairy.com
FEATURES	7 Rooms and 1 Suite; Private & shared baths	Children welcome	Pets not allowed; Resident outdoor cats & farm animals	Handicapped accessible	Will accommodate guests' special dietary needs

The Inn at Celebrity Dairy welcomes you to the peace and comfort of an old home-place and the purposeful life of a 300-acre working dairy in rural Chatham County. A community gathering place for over a century, Celebrity Dairy now extends its warm welcome and informal comfort to guests year-round.

Wake refreshed to join the farm crew for a breakfast of (naturally) chèvre (goat cheese) omelets or home-baked pastries, along with seasonal fruits and preserves from the neighboring gardens.

Caramelized Onion & Goat Cheese Omelet

Yield: 6 servings

"We serve this rustic country omelet on a large platter with roasted potatoes. The omelette is good served cold or hot, or try slicing it into thin shreds and using it as a salad topping."—Innkeeper

 4 Tbsp canola oil, divided
 2 large onions, chopped
12 large eggs
 2 Tbsp water or milk
 4 oz. goat cheese, crumbled
   Lemon pepper and black pepper, to taste
   Fresh herbs, for garnish

Heat 2 tablespoons of oil in a skillet over medium-low heat. Add onions and cook until golden. Turn heat to low and cook, stirring occasionally, for 30–45 minutes, until well caramelized (golden brown and sweet).

In a bowl, beat eggs and water until frothy and light yellow. Heat remaining 2 tablespoons of oil in an omelet pan over medium heat until oil is almost smoking. Add eggs. As eggs cook, lift edges of omelet and let uncooked eggs flow underneath and come in contact with pan.

Turn heat to low and sprinkle caramelized onions and goat cheese over half of eggs. Season with lemon pepper and black pepper. Release eggs from pan (use a spatula, if needed) and fold uncovered half of eggs over onions and goat cheese. Cover and let stand at low heat or off the heat until eggs are set. Invert a serving plate over pan, then invert pan and turn omelet out onto plate, bottom-side-up. Garnish with fresh herbs and serve.

Inn at Iris Meadows B&B

INNKEEPERS   George & Becky Fain

ADDRESS   304 Love Lane, Waynesville, NC 28786

TELEPHONE   828-456-3877 | 888-466-4747 (Inn-Iris) | Fax 828-456-3847

CONTACT   IrisMeadows@aol.com | www.irismeadows.com

FEATURES   7 Rooms; Private baths | Children age 12 and older welcome | Pets welcome (limited), resident dog and cat | Will accommodate guests' special dietary needs

*"We came for a few days and wanted to
spend the rest of our lives here."*—Guest

Step back into a gentler time and experience the romantic elegance and grandeur of the beautifully restored Inn … where cool summers, colorful mountain autumns, mild winters, and lush springs blend with southern hospitality and small town charm to welcome you. Located in the heart of the Great Smoky Mountains, the Inn is nestled amidst five rolling acres overlooking the picturesque town of Waynesville.

Enjoy glorious breakfasts by the fire in the dining room, or on the veranda, weather permitting. Savor freshly brewed coffee or tea with mid-afternoon refreshments on the porches or in the parlors. Select

from seven romantic, elegantly appointed guest rooms—with glowing fireplaces, private chandeliered baths with luxurious double whirlpool tubs, heavenly king or queen beds, air conditioning, and intriguing antiques.

Mountain Mornings Granola Parfait

Yield: 12–14 half-cup servings

"This recipe is a favorite among our guests. Even guests who were not granola fans prior to this dish ask for it when they return."—Innkeeper

3 cups uncooked regular old fashioned oats
¼ cup wheat germ
¼ cup wheat bran
½ tsp cinnamon
¼ cup sunflower seed kernels
½ cup pecan pieces
½ cup sliced almonds
¼ cup flaked sweet coconut (optional)
2 Tbsp sesame seeds

½ cup butter
½ cup firmly packed brown sugar
2 Tbsp light corn syrup (Karo)
1 tsp vanilla extract
1 cup mixed dried fruit such as chopped dates, golden and brown raisins, dried cranberries, dried cherries

Preheat oven to 350°F. Combine first 9 ingredients in a large bowl. Set oats mixture aside. Cook butter and brown sugar in a medium saucepan over medium heat, stirring constantly, until butter is melted and sugar is dissolved. Stir in corn syrup. Remove from heat and stir in vanilla. Pour sugar mixture evenly over oats mixture, tossing to coat well. Spread mixture evenly in a lightly greased jelly-roll or broiler pan.

Bake for 25–30 minutes, stirring 3 times at 7-minute intervals. Set the oven timer to stir every 7 minutes—we cook it for 28 minutes, which works perfectly in our ovens. Cool completely on wire rack; stir often while cooling. (Lack of stirring may result in one huge granola bar!)

Stir in dried fruit when you are ready to serve it to preserve the crispness of the granola. Store in airtight container for up to 2 weeks. (It never lasts that long here, so we can't guarantee shelf life!)

For parfait, serve layered with vanilla yogurt, fresh fruit and berries in a parfait glass. Garnish with fresh mint sprigs.

INN ON MAIN STREET B&B

INNKEEPERS	Nancy & Dan Ward
ADDRESS	88 S Main Street, Weaverville, NC 28787
TELEPHONE	828-645-4935 | 977-873-6074
CONTACT	relax@innonmain.com | www.innonmain.com
FEATURES	7 Rooms; Private baths | Children age 12 and older welcome | No pets | Will accommodate guests' special dietary needs

Inn on Main Street B&B is among the best of Asheville's Inns, but located in quaint, artsy Weaverville. Our Inn is a good choice for girlfriend getaways, romantic rooms, spa specials, or visiting the Biltmore Estate. Each of our rooms is unique and include twin, king, queen, or full-size beds. Some have fireplaces and whirlpool tubs. All of our rooms have wireless Internet, cable TV with DVD or VCR, and quality amenities. Walk to downtown Weaverville and visit nearby cafes, spa services, galleries, live music and other entertainment.

Western North Carolina is a mecca for outdoor enthusiasts. There are thousands of miles of trophy trout streams joining rivers where whitewater rafters and kayakers can take in the mountain beauty up close. Where highland valleys meet climbing hills, some of the most beautiful golf courses in the nation challenge all skill levels, and Inn guests get a discount at Reems Creek Golf Club, which is one of the best.

Dan's Almost-Famous Frittata

Yield: 2 servings

"Frittatas in Italy are a Friday supper dish, a way to use up leftover pasta and veggies from the previous week. We set out to have a signature dish when we opened the inn, and decided to serve a different variation on the frittata every day. We soon had guests tell us they loved the frittatas, but couldn't we just serve pancakes or something else after a couple days? What were we thinking? This potato version remains very popular, but we serve it only once during a guest's stay."—Innkeeper

1   medium to large red potato
1   Tbsp onion, chopped
1   Tbsp bell pepper, chopped
1   Tbsp canola oil, divided
½   tsp fresh chopped rosemary
    pinch of salt and pepper
3   eggs, beaten
2   thin slices fresh tomato
2   Tbsp grated Parmesan cheese

Microwave potato 4 minutes on high, then dice. Sauté onions and peppers in a 6-inch cast iron pan (or other oven-ready pan) with half the oil, and set aside. Fry potatoes with remaining oil and spices. Potatoes can be kept on low heat for an hour if need be. A few minutes before serving, add peppers and onions to pan and cover with beaten eggs. Float tomato slices on top, and sprinkle Parmesan over all. Cook on medium heat until sides of frittata gel. To finish, put pan under broiler a few minutes until top of frittata resembles a pizza. Cut frittata in half and check to make sure center is firm. Serve hot.

THE INN ON MILL CREEK

INNKEEPERS	Brigette & Dave Walters
ADDRESS	3895 Mill Creek Road, Old Fort, NC 28762
TELEPHONE	828-668-1115
CONTACT	info@innonmillcreek.com | www.innonmillcreek.com
FEATURES	7 Rooms; Private baths | Children welcome (2 family friendly rooms) | Pets welcome (2 pet friendly rooms) | Gluten-free, vegan and vegetarian options, as well as alternatives for other specific food sensitivities available | Limited handicap accessability (please call) |

The Inn on Mill Creek is tucked away in a private, wooded setting two miles inside Pisgah National Forest, 25 minutes east of Asheville, and 10 minutes northeast of the town of Black Mountain. A pond, fruit orchard, and berry bushes are part of the Inn's seven-plus acres, and the property is one of a handful of privately owned sites on the extensive North Carolina Birding Trail—Mountain Region, as well as a Certified Wildlife Habitat.

Inside the Inn, each of the seven contemporary guest rooms reflects the natural beauty of North Carolina's mountains and forests in color and style, and several rooms have double-jetted tubs and fireplaces for unwinding and relaxing. A two-story Great Room common area with a vaulted rough-hewn cedar ceiling adds to the Inn's comfortable, nature-inspired style. A full breakfast is served in the sunny solarium in warm weather months and inside the Main House dining area in cool weather. *Our State* magazine featured our breakfast fare in February 2012.

Pumpkin Belgian Waffles

Yield: 7 Belgian Waffles

Dry Ingredients:

  1   cup all-purpose flour
1¼   cups self-rising flour
  ¼   cup cornstarch
  2   tsp baking powder
  ½   tsp baking soda
1½   tsp ground cinnamon
  1   tsp ground allspice
  ½   tsp salt
  ½   tsp ground ginger

Wet Ingredients:

  4   large eggs, separated
  4   Tbsp butter, melted
  2   Tbsp vegetable oil
²/₃   cup cooked, mashed pumpkin
  ¼   cup brown sugar
  1   cup 2% milk
  1   cup buttermilk
  2   tsp vanilla

Egg Whites:

  4   egg whites, beaten to soft peaks
  1   tsp white sugar (add while beating whites)

Sift together dry ingredients in a large bowl. In a separate bowl, whisk together egg yolks (save the egg whites), then one at a time whisk in the butter, oil, pumpkin, brown sugar, milk, buttermilk, and vanilla. Add to the flour mixture, stirring just until moistened. Prepare the egg whites and sugar. Gently fold egg whites into batter until mostly combined. Cook in Belgian waffle iron; will take slightly longer than for other batters. Do not overfill griddle plates.

THE IVY B&B

INNKEEPERS	Jerry & Ellen Roth
ADDRESS	331 North Main Street, Warrenton, NC 27589
TELEPHONE	800-919-9886 | 252-257-9300
CONTACT	info@ivybedandbreakfast.com | www.ivybedandbreakfast.com
FEATURES	4 Rooms; 3 Private baths (the Ivy Suite consists of 2 rooms connected by adjoining bath | Children over 6 years of age welcome | No pets (nearby kennel available with prior arrangement)

The Ivy is an elegant bed and breakfast establishment in the historic district of Warrenton. The Inn is located near Lake Gaston and the Kerr Lake reservoir, and a short drive from Richmond, Virginia, and Raleigh, North Carolina. The Ivy is just a leisurely stroll to quaint downtown antique and specialty shops, Hardware Café, historic churches, and the courthouse square on Main Street, USA.

Features include fireplaces, heart pine floors, lots of stained glass, antiques, and lovely Waverly window and bed treatments. Equipped with modern conveniences without losing its charm and character, the 1903 Queen Anne home has undergone an extensive restoration.

Stuffed French Toast

Yield: 6 servings

"We use French bread for this recipe—you can get it pre-sliced or slice your own. If we slice it, we usually slice it a little thinner."—Innkeeper

1	stick butter (½ cup)
1	cup brown sugar
¼	cup maple syrup
⅓	cup chopped walnuts and pecans
12	Slices bread—French or cinnamon raisin
	cream cheese
	dried fruit bits
6	eggs
1½	cups milk
1	tsp vanilla

Plan ahead—this dish needs overnight refrigeration.

Place the butter, brown sugar and maple syrup in a glass bowl. Microwave only until the butter is melted (45 to 60 seconds). Stir to dissolve the sugar and mix ingredients well. Pour this mixture into a 9x12-inch baking dish. Sprinkle nuts over this mixture.

If french bread is not precut, slices should be a little thicker than a regular bread slice.

Spread softened cream cheese on half of the bread slices. Place the fruit bits on top of the bread slices. Top with the plain bread slices to make a "sandwich." (Cut in half diagonally if using regular sized bread.) Place the bread in the baking dish—do not overlap slices.

In a bowl, mix the eggs, milk, and vanilla. Pour mixture over the bread. Cover the dish and refrigerate overnight. In the morning, preheat oven to 350°F. Remove dish from refrigerator and bake for about 45 minutes, uncovered. To serve, flip toast over onto a plate so the syrup side is up.

THE KING'S DAUGHTERS INN

INNKEEPERS	Colin & Deanna Crossman
ADDRESS	204 N. Buchanan Blvd., Durham, NC 27701-2009
TELEPHONE	919-354-7000	877-534-8534	Fax 866-489-2029
CONTACT	info@thekingsdaughtersinn.com	www.thekingsdaughtersinn.com
FEATURES	17 Rooms; Private baths	Children welcome (in the 2-room suites)	No pets (can recommend quality local boarding options)

The King's Daughters Inn began a new chapter of its history in April 2009, after being transformed into a seventeen-room boutique B&B. Built in the 1920s, the home provided dormitory-style housing for single, aging women. After closing its doors in 2006, the new owners marshaled the 17,000 sq. ft. building through an extensive green renovation to create the luxurious inn that stands here today.

The King's Daughters Inn offers the amenities of a first-class hotel with the intimacy of a B&B. Enjoy high-speed wireless Internet throughout, ample event and meeting space, and spacious common areas for relaxing and socializing. All rooms feature the same full slate of amenities including luxurious robes; triple-sheeted beds; locally produced, all-natural toiletries; flat-screen HDTVs; and individual climate control. Savor gourmet breakfasts, afternoon tea, and evening wine and scotch. Let our concierge share an insider's opinions on the best restaurants and activities Durham has to offer ... and then borrow one of our bicycles to get there in style!

Cheesy Creamy Hashbrowns

Yield: 10 servings

1 pkg. shredded Simply Potatoes (in dairy section at grocery store)
½ cup melted butter (1 stick)
1 cup sour cream
1 can cream of mushroom soup
1 large onion, diced
1 cup grated cheddar cheese, divided
½ cup grated Monterey Jack cheese

Preheat oven to 350°F. Mix all ingredients together in a large bowl (reserve ½ cup cheddar for topping) and pour into 9x13-inch baking dish. Sprinkle with rest of the cheddar. Bake for 40–50 minutes. Should be bubbly around edges and lightly browned.

Monterey Jack cheese is named after its creator, David Jacks, a nineteenth-century cheesemaker who resided near Monterey, California.

LAKE SHORE LODGE

INNKEEPERS	Ted & Phyllis Russ
ADDRESS	2014 Lake Shore Drive, Lake Waccamaw, NC 28450
TELEPHONE	910-646-3748
CONTACT	phiz@embarqmail.com | www.lakewaccamawbandb.com
FEATURES	3 Rooms; Private baths | No pets | Wireless Internet

Lake Waccamaw, the best-kept secret in North Carolina. This beautiful lake, nestled in a sleepy little village, is a lure to vacationers who like the serenity of peace and quiet in old-fashioned surroundings. Historically, this was a lodge where hunters and fishermen came yearly to enjoy the out-of-doors. Today, it is an artist's delight with a second-story sun porch (decorated like an old-fashioned soda parlor) overlooking the lake. The breathtaking sunsets glow on the horizon and set the lake afire with color.

Inside, the warmth of antiques and Southern hospitality await your pleasure as you read or play the piano in the Music Room, lounge in the Great Room or rock on the screened-in porch. Guests are welcome to sit on the dock and feed the ducks, wet a hook, soak up the sun, or just enjoy the spectacular view of the lake surrounded by woods.

Fruit Slush

Yield: 24 servings

"My most requested recipe—sooo refreshing."—Innkeeper

1 (6-oz.) can frozen lemonade
1 (6-oz.) can frozen orange juice
1 small box frozen strawberries
1 large can crushed pineapple with juice
3 or more bananas (lemonade keeps from turning dark)
1 cup sugar melted in 1 cup warm water

Combine all ingredients in a 9x12-inch cake pan, and place in freezer. Before serving, remove from freezer and allow to thaw 10–15 minutes, then chop out hunks and place in sherbet dishes. Freeze remainder to be used another day.

Bananas are one fruit that develops better flavor when ripened off the tree. To ripen, keep uncovered at room temperature. For speedy ripening, enclose bananas in a perforated brown paper bag.

THE LAMPLIGHT INN

INNKEEPER	Shirley Payne
ADDRESS	1680 Flemingtown Road, Henderson, NC 27537
TELEPHONE	252-438-6311 | 877-222-0100 | Fax 252-438-6311
CONTACT	inn@lamplightbnb.net | www.lamplightbnb.net
FEATURES	4 Rooms; Private baths | Children welcome | Pets welcome (call for room availability), 2 resident outside cats | Will accommodate guests' special dietary needs

Step back from the fast pace of today, and join us by the fire in the parlor. Located 45 minutes from the Raleigh-Durham airport and less than 2 miles from Interstate 85, The Lamplight Inn resides on a 150-year-old, 5-acre tobacco farm. Let us beckon you with the soft glow of the many chimney lamps used to light this restored farm. Relax on the wraparound porch, in the corncrib-screened gazebo, or stroll the grounds and explore the tobacco curing barns, the yoga platform in the woods, or the labyrinth.

A short drive will bring you to the Kerr Lake State Recreation Area to enjoy sailing, fishing, water skiing, and hiking. This 50,000-acre, man-made lake is a haven for water sports enthusiasts and landlubbers alike. More than 800 miles of wooded shoreline provide access to a variety of fun-filled activities on the lake.

Festive Oyster Casserole

Yield: 12 servings

"This has been my Christmas Eve dish for years. I love sharing it with friends because it is so special." —Innkeeper

1 quart oysters, drained
16 soda crackers, crushed
1 (10-oz.) pkg. frozen chopped spinach, thawed and drained
1 cup chopped celery
½ cup chopped onion
1 (4-oz.) jar pimentos, chopped
¼ cup lemon juice
½ tsp paprika
1 Tbsp Worcestershire sauce
1 tsp salt
Buttered cracker crumbs, for topping

Preheat oven to 350°F. Toss together all ingredients, except buttered cracker crumbs, in a casserole dish or a 9x13-inch baking dish. Top with buttered cracker crumbs. Bake for 30 minutes.

THE LODGE ON LAKE LURE

INNKEEPER	Gisela Hopke
ADDRESS	361 Charlotte Drive, Lake Lure, NC 28746
TELEPHONE	828-625-2789 | 800-733-2785
CONTACT	info@lodgeonlakelure.com | www.lodgeonlakelure.com
FEATURES	17 Rooms; Private baths | Children age 8 and older welcome | No pets, resident cat | Handicap accessible | Will accommodate guests' special dietary needs

Along the shores of majestic Lake Lure, you can golf, hike, boat, fish, ride horses, or just lounge and be spoiled at The Lodge at Lake Lure. An elegant getaway, the lodge is furnished with art, antiques, and collectibles and offers fabulous views, stone fireplaces, terraces and distinctive dining.

The lodge is a wonderful combination of an elegant country inn and a casual bed & breakfast—an intimate environment with all the privacy you want. It is a large, rambling structure situated high on the hillside to afford a sweeping view of the lake and beyond.

Mark's Marinated Quail with Basil-Infused Honey

Yield: 4 to 8 servings

4–8 European boned quail (partially boned)
½ medium yellow onion, sliced into half rounds
2 cloves garlic
1–2 sprigs fresh rosemary
1 bay leaf
4–6 black peppercorns
¼ cup balsamic vinegar
Extra-virgin olive oil
Salt and black pepper, to taste
¼ cup clover honey
¼ cup hot water
8–10 fresh basil leaves
¾ tsp crushed red pepper flakes

Place quail in a small baking dish. Combine onion, garlic, rosemary, bay leaf, peppercorns, balsamic vinegar and enough olive oil to cover quail; pour over quail, cover, and refrigerate for at least 4 hours and up to 24 hours.

Preheat oven to 350°F. Remove quail from marinade; shake off excess marinade. Season with salt and pepper, then sear both sides of quail in a skillet (or on a grill) over high heat. Transfer quail to oven and roast for 10–12 minutes, or until cooked through.

While quail are roasting, combine honey, water, basil and red pepper flakes in a small saucepan over medium-low heat. Cook for 10–12 minutes (be careful not to burn honey), then strain. When quail are done, let rest for several minutes, then glaze with honey mixture. Serve 2 quail per person, with mushroom risotto and asparagus as an entrée or 1 quail per person, with blue cheese-stuffed roasted red bliss potatoes as an appetizer.

Lois Jane's Riverview Inn

INNKEEPER	Gladis Ozmon
ADDRESS	106 West Bay Street, Southport, NC 28461
TELEPHONE	910-457-6701
CONTACT	riverviewinn@ec.rr.com	www.loisjanes.com
FEATURES	4 Rooms; 1 Suite; Private & shared baths	Children age 12 and older welcome	No pets	Will accommodate guests' special dietary needs

L ois Jane's Riverview Inn is owned and operated by fourth generation, direct descendants of the builder. Constructed in 1891, the home was faithfully restored in 1995 and furnished with traditional period furniture and accessories, many of which are family heirlooms.

Enjoy the breeze on the riverside porches while watching the ships go by. Stroll along the River Walk to antique shops, restaurants, the North Carolina Maritime Museum, and other interesting sites in this quaint little town that was settled more than 200 years ago.

Nana's Belgian Waffles

Yield: 4 servings

"These waffles are a winner. The recipe has been handed down from generation to generation." —Innkeeper

4 large eggs, separated
3 Tbsp butter, melted and cooled
½ tsp vanilla extract
1 cup all-purpose flour
½ tsp salt
   Whipped cream, for serving
1 cup sliced strawberries, for serving

In a medium bowl, beat egg yolks. Mix in butter and vanilla. In a small bowl, combine flour and salt; add to egg yolk mixture and mix well. In a separate bowl, beat egg whites until stiff peaks form; fold into egg yolk mixture. Bake in a preheated Belgian waffle iron until golden brown. Serve with whipped cream and strawberries.

MOREHEAD MANOR B&B

INNKEEPERS	Daniel & Monica Edwards
ADDRESS	914 Vickers Avenue, Durham, NC 27701-3145
TELEPHONE	919-687-4366 | Fax 919-687-4245
CONTACT	info@moreheadmanor.com | www.moreheadmanor.com
FEATURES	4 Rooms; 1 Suite; 4 Private baths | Children age 12 and older welcome (unless the party rents the entire facility) | No pets, resident Siamese cats | Will accommodate guests' special dietary needs

Built in 1910 for the CEO of Liggett and Meyers, this splendidly decorated 8,000-square-foot Colonial Revival–style home is located within walking distance of downtown, the Durham Bulls Ballpark, and historic Brightleaf Square.

A place where elegance, excitement, and hospitality meet, guests can spend the afternoon listening to music, having tea, or enjoying a good book in any of the Inn's common areas. A full breakfast, complimentary beverages, and scrumptious homemade desserts are offered each day.

Mom's Seafood Casserole

Yield: 6 to 8 servings

"A childhood favorite that I have been able to pass on for my guests to enjoy."—Innkeeper

½ stick butter, melted
1 cup chopped onion
1 medium green bell pepper, chopped
½ cup chopped celery
½ cup wild rice, cooked according to package directions
½ cup white rice, cooked according to package directions
1 lb. shrimp, cooked
6 oz. crabmeat with juice
2 (10¾-oz.) cans cream of mushroom soup
¼ cup water
1 (4-oz.) can sliced mushrooms, drained
1 (2-oz.) jar pimentos, drained
1 cup Pepperidge Farms stuffing mix

Preheat oven to 350°F. Grease a 9x13-inch baking dish. Melt butter in a large skillet over medium heat. Add onion, bell pepper and celery; cook until soft. Add remaining ingredients, except stuffing, and stir to combine. Place mixture in baking dish, sprinkle with stuffing and bake for 1 hour.

MORNING GLORY INN

INNKEEPERS	Betsy & Michael Grannis
ADDRESS	507 E. Second Street, Clayton, NC 27520
TELEPHONE	919-550-8547 | Fax 919-550-8611
CONTACT	info@morning-glory-inn.com | www.morning-glory-inn.com
FEATURES	5 Rooms; Private baths | Children welcome | No pets | Will accommodate guest's special dietary needs

Welcome to Clayton's unique and authentic B&B located right in the heart of town. The Morning Glory Inn is a magnificent 6,400 square foot Victorian that was built in 1907. Each room is delightfully decorated with a specific floral theme, comfortable sitting areas and inviting queen- or king-size beds. We offer a full gourmet breakfast with a selection of down-home morsels.

Our Inn has several seating areas allowing our guests to gather in a choice of cozy settings outside of their rooms. For those who enjoy the outdoors, our lovely wraparound porch with ceiling fan looks out over the front and side yards of our Inn. Relax while listening to the abundance of birds chirping. You can also enjoy strolling around our gardens. There are quaint areas to sit and enjoy the beautiful foliage and the serene setting that surrounds you.

Apple Danish Pastry

Yield: 12–24 servings

Pastry:

    3 cups flour
    ½ tsp salt
    1 cup shortening
    1 egg yolk (save egg white)
    ½ cup milk

Filling:

    2 (3-oz.) pkg. cream cheese, softened
    3 Tbsp sugar
    1 egg
    1 can Apple Pie Filling

Glaze:

    1 egg white, beaten lightly
    ½ cup powdered sugar
  2–3 tsp water

Preheat oven to 375°F. In large bowl, combine flour and salt; cut in shortening until mixture resembles coarse crumbs. Add egg yolk and milk, stir well. Divide pastry dough in half. Roll half of dough to 10x15 inches. Transfer dough to same size pan. Set aside. In small bowl, combine cream cheese and sugar; beat until smooth. Add egg and beat well. Spread mixture evenly over rolled pastry. Spoon apple pie filling over pastry. Roll second half of pastry to fit pan; place over filling, sealing edges. Paint with some of the beaten egg white. Bake 35 minutes or until golden brown. Mix glaze. Drizzle over warm pastry. Cut into serving sizes.

THE MOSS HOUSE B&B

INNKEEPERS	Rebecca & Scott Sipprell
ADDRESS	129 Van Norden Street, Washington, NC 27889
TELEPHONE	252-975-3967
CONTACT	info@themosshouse.com	www.themosshouse.com
FEATURES	4 Rooms; Private baths	Children age 6 and older welcome	No pets, resident dog	Will accommodate guests' special dietary needs

Built in 1902, The Moss House offers the gracious style of days gone by with a modern and eclectic attitude. Modern amenities include central AC, "green" high-quality bath amenities, flatscreen TVs with DVD players in each room, and free WI-FI. We are in the heart of the Historic District, near shops and restaurants, one block from the Pamlico River and at the hub of many adventurous forays. Kick back on our wide veranda and enjoy the garden or rent a kayak and cruise the vast estuary system.

Our full breakfast each morning includes our own Moss House blend of coffee, roasted for us in Rocky Mount, NC. Each breakfast includes fresh fruit, baked goods made in house, and an entrée to please your palette. We shop local and include local farm produce as much as we can.

Orange French Toast

Yield: 4 or 5 slices—You can easily double this!

"I enjoyed developing this from combining several recipe ideas and finding my own twist! Cooking should be about putting ourselves into a dish."—Innkeeper

- 1   loaf Hawaiian Bread (found in the deli area) or Challah bread
- 2   Tbsp sugar
- ⅓   cup all-purpose flour
- ¼   tsp salt
-     Pinch grated nutmeg
- 1   large egg
- 2   Tbsp unsalted butter, melted
- ¾   cup milk (or part half & half)
- 1   tsp vanilla extract
- 1   tsp orange extract (or Grand Marnier)
- 1   tsp or more of grated orange peel

Preheat oven to 325°F. Slice bread into one inch slices (four slices for this recipe). Put on a baking sheet with a rack and dry in the oven for about four minutes per side. This dryer bread is the secret to the French toast!

Whisk together the dry ingredients. In a separate bowl, whisk egg and beat in melted butter, then add milk, extracts and peel. Whisk the dry ingredients into the wet.

Preheat a large skillet or a griddle for 5 minutes. Pour batter into a 9x11-inch casserole dish, lay the pieces of bread, in batches, into the batter and let it sit a minute, flip and let excess batter drip off. Swirl a bit of butter on the hot griddle and lay on the French toast. Cook for about 4 minutes and turn for 4 more minutes. Keep warm in 250°F oven while cooking the other slices. Serve with fresh berries and warm maple syrup.

OAKLAND COTTAGE B&B

INNKEEPERS	Mary & Byron Bridges
ADDRESS	74 Oakland Road, Asheville, NC 28801
TELEPHONE	828-994-2627 | 866-858-0863
CONTACT	info@VacationInAsheville.com | www.vacationinasheville.com
FEATURES	2 Rooms; 3 Suites; Private baths | Children welcome |
	Pets welcome (limited) | Wireless Internet

Oakland Cottage B&B has a convenient in-town location, 1.5 miles from the entrance of the Biltmore Estate and downtown Asheville. Ambience abounds in this 1910 Arts & Crafts–style "Cottage." Reserve a suite or a room: each of the three suites has two rooms, en suite bath, robes, hairdryer, soaps and shampoos, coffee maker, cable TV, some with mini-fridge, microwave, and private deck. We also have 2 great value rooms: The Rose Rooms. Each of the Rose Rooms has our standard amenities described above at great value. Or, reserve the whole Cottage (excepting the innkeeper's apartment).

With a capacity for up to 20 guests, Oakland Cottage is perfect for family and friend gatherings, girlfriend getaways, wedding groups, and small retreat-style meetings. Large common areas provide additional indoor and outdoor guest space, as well as added conveniences, including a guest kitchenette and guest-use laundry room.

MeMaw's Cranberry Apple Casserole

Yield: 6 servings

Filling

 1 cup unpeeled chopped apples
 ½ cup raw cranberries
 1–2 Tbsp sugar

Topping

 1 cup cooking oats (not quick)
 ⅓ cup brown sugar or maple syrup
 ⅓ cup melted butter or margarine
 ¼ cup flour
 ¼ cup chopped nuts

Preheat oven to 350°F. Lightly spray a 2-quart baking dish. Combine "filling" ingredients and spread in baking dish. Mix together "topping" ingredients and spread topping over filling. Bake for about 45 minutes to 1 hour. Serve warm, but also good cold.

OLD NORTH DURHAM INN

INNKEEPERS	Debbie & Jim Vickery
ADDRESS	922 North Mangum Street, Durham, NC 27701
TELEPHONE	919-683-1885
CONTACT	ondi@nc.rr.com | www.bbonline.com/nc/oldnorth
FEATURES	3 Rooms; Private baths | Children welcome | No pets | Wireless Internet

Visitors to the Old North Durham Inn are invited to share in the charm of this historic, Prairie Foursquare home. The Inn is listed in Preservation Durham's Inventory of Historic Properties and is a recipient of an "Architectural Conservation Citation" for its renovations. It is located in one of Durham's historic residential neighborhoods, just a mile north of Durham's Downtown Entertainment District and a mile east of Duke University, with easy access to major highways.

The Inn offers 3 large, second floor guest rooms featuring high ceilings, central heat/air, ceiling fans, queen-size beds, period wall covering and furnishings, sitting areas, desks, WI-FI, flatscreen TVs with DVD players, stereos, and en suite baths. The wraparound porch is a perfect place to enjoy an early morning cup of coffee or a homemade treat from the ever-stocked cookie jar. The downstairs parlor, with its

coffered ceiling, beautiful oak floors, fireplace, large flat-screen TV with DVD player, and music center is a perfect place to meet other guests or relax with family and friends.

Phyllis's Ginger Cookies

Yield: about 4 dozen cookies

"This is a staple of my husband's Maine family. The cookies come out so round and perfect, guests think they are store-bought, until they bite into them."—Innkeeper

¾ cup shortening (½ vegetable shortening; ½ margarine)
1 cup sugar
1 beaten egg
¼ cup molasses
2 cups unsifted flour
3 tsp baking soda
½ tsp salt
1 tsp ground cinnamon
1 tsp ground cloves
1 tsp ground ginger

Preheat oven to 350°F. Cream together shortening, sugar, egg, and molasses. Stir in flour, soda and spices. Roll dough into small 1-inch balls. Bake on ungreased cookie sheet for 12 to 15 minutes. Cookies should be crinkly and soft on top when you take them from the oven.

Pamlico House B&B

INNKEEPER	Virginia Finnerty
ADDRESS	400 East Main Street, Washington, NC 27889
TELEPHONE	252-946-5001
CONTACT	info@PamlicoHouseBB.com | www.PamlicoHouseBB.com
FEATURES	5 Rooms; Private baths | Children age 6 and older welcome | No pets, resident tiny shy Yorkie | Will accommodate guests' special dietary needs

Located in Washington's Historic District, the Pamlico House was built by St. Peter's Episcopal Church as a rectory in 1906. The large Colonial Revival–style frame house is just a short walk from downtown Washington, the river walk and the public boat docks, the Estuarium, and Main Street shops, including an ice cream parlor, restaurants, and bars.

Whether you're visiting Washington for business or pleasure, we'll cater our 5-star service to your needs, including fresh flowers, luxurious bathrobes and slippers, luxurious all-natural toiletries, hair dryer, iron and ironing boards, alarm clocks, extra pillows and blankets, and even spa services upon request.

Fruit Pancakes

Yield: 8–10 pancakes

"When I started getting repeat guests I worried about serving them the same breakfast so asked several of them what they thought. All answered the same, they don't have breakfast like the Pamlico House breakfast at home and look forward to it when they come, so please don't change it."—Innkeeper

1½ cup flour
3 Tbsp sugar
2 tsp baking powder
1½ tsp Kosher salt
½ cup sour cream
¾ cup + 1 Tbsp milk
2 extra large eggs at room temp
1 tsp vanilla
1 tsp lemon zest
  unsalted butter
  seasonal fruit (bananas, blueberries, apples)
  maple syrup

Sift together flour, sugar, baking powder and salt. In a separate bowl lightly beat sour cream, milk, eggs, vanilla and lemon zest. Add the wet ingredients to the dry ones mixing only until combined.

Melt 1 tablespoon unsalted butter in a large skillet over medium-low heat until it bubbles. Ladle batter into pan using ¼ cup measure. Distribute 3–5 fruit slices on top of each pancake. Cook 2–3 minutes until bubbles appear on top and the underside is nicely browned. Flip and cook for another minute, until browned. Wipe pan with paper towel, add more butter and continue cooking until all batter is used.

The pancakes will stay warm in a preheated 200°F oven for 15–20 minutes. Serve garnished with sliced fruit and sprinkled with powdered sugar and maple syrup.

Rosemary House B&B

INNKEEPERS Karen & Mac Pullen

ADDRESS 76 West Street, Pittsboro, NC 27312

TELEPHONE 919-542-5515 | 888-643-2017

CONTACT karen@rosemary-bb.com | www.rosemary-bb.com

FEATURES 5 Rooms; Private baths | Children welcome | No pets | Will accommodate guests' special dietary needs | Wireless Internet

Welcome to the Rosemary House B&B, a gracious 1912 Colonial Revival house listed on the National Register of Historic Places. The Inn is located in historic Pittsboro, near Chapel Hill and convenient to Raleigh and Durham.

All guest rooms have free wireless high-speed Internet connection, ceiling fan, air conditioning, telephone, private bathroom with tub and shower, flatscreen cable TV, iron and ironing board, hair dryer, toiletries, and shower cap. Bottled water is available in the upstairs hall fridge. A full breakfast is served in the dining room at the time of your choosing. Entrées may include vegetarian eggs Benedict, huevos

rancheros, Belgian waffles, or herb omelets accompanied by rosemary-roasted potatoes. For healthy eaters, oatmeal with apples, pecans, and raisins is always offered.

Apricot Pecan Muffins

Yield: 12 Muffins

"These muffins are delicious and moist. They also freeze well."—Innkeeper

    2 cups whole-wheat pastry flour (or white pastry flour)
    ½ cup sugar
    1 tsp baking soda
    ¼ tsp salt
    1 cup plain yogurt
    ¼ cup milk
    ¼ cup canola oil
    1 large egg, beaten
    2 Tbsp maple syrup
    1 tsp vanilla extract
    ¾ cup chopped dried apricots
    ½ cup chopped pecans

Preheat oven to 350°F. Spray muffin cups with nonstick cooking spray. In a large bowl, mix flour, sugar, baking soda, and salt. In a medium bowl, mix yogurt, milk, oil, egg, maple syrup, and vanilla. Make a well in center of flour mixture. Add yogurt mixture to well and stir just to combine. Stir in apricots and pecans. Spoon batter into muffin cups. Bake for 20 minutes. Remove muffins from oven and cool for 5 minutes in pan, then remove from pan.

THE SUNSET INN

INNKEEPERS	Andrea Ward & Dave Nelson
ADDRESS	9 North Shore Drive E, Sunset Beach, NC 28468
TELEPHONE	910-575-1000 | 888-575-1001 | Fax 910-579-1018
CONTACT	info@thesunsetinn.net | www.thesunsetinn.net
FEATURES	14 Rooms; Private baths | Children age 12 and older welcome | No pets | Will accommodate guests' special dietary needs

"For the Sunset Inn, the third time was even more charming than the first two. It really is like staying in the room of a friend's Southern plantation. What other accommodation gives you outdoor showers to rinse off after the beach and your own storage room to stow your rented bikes?"—Trip Advisor

Our picturesque island has a temperate climate without the brutal extremes of summer or winter. Development in the area is limited and our natural beach is unspoiled and uncrowded, the way nature intended a beach to be. Sunset Beach offers one of the widest beaches on the East Coast with white fine-grained sand that soothes your senses.

Our ten standard rooms and four grand rooms begin a long list of comforts crafted especially for our guests' peace of mind. Beautifully appointed rooms with king-sized beds, private baths, private screened porches, wet bars, large community porches, and private storage areas for bikes, golf clubs, beach chairs, etc., all combine to create a relaxed atmosphere that most can only dream about.

Green Chile & Cheese Breakfast Casserole

Yield: 8–10 servings

15 eggs
 3 egg whites
 ¾ cup flour
1½ tsp baking powder
 2 (8-oz.) cans diced green chiles
 1 quart & 1 pint (40-oz.) cottage cheese
 1 cup (8-oz.) cream cheese, softened
24 oz. shredded Monterey Jack cheese
    Salt and pepper to taste

Preheat oven to 350°F. Beat eggs and egg whites lightly in a large bowl. Stir in flour, baking powder, chiles, all cheeses, salt and pepper. Mix well. Pour mixture into greased 11x15-inch baking pan. Bake for about 40 minutes or until casserole is set.

For a 9x13-inch pan

10 eggs
 2 egg whites
 ½ cup flour
 1 tsp baking powder
 2 (8-oz.) cans diced green chiles
 1 quart (24-oz.) cottage cheese
 ½ cup (4-oz.) cream cheese, softened
16 oz. shredded Monterey Jack cheese
    Salt and pepper to taste

THE TROTT HOUSE INN

INNKEEPER	Anne Stedman
ADDRESS	802 North Main Avenue, Newton, NC 28658
TELEPHONE	828-465-0404 | 877-435-7994
CONTACT	rents40@aol.com | www.trotthouse.com
FEATURES	4 Rooms; 1 Suite; Private baths | Children age 12 and older welcome | No pets, resident dog | Will accommodate guests' special dietary needs

Located in Newton, the county seat of Catawba County, The Trott House Inn gives guests a chance to enjoy such local attractions as the Blue Ridge Parkway and the Hickory Furniture Mart and Hickory Antiques Mall with over 100 retailers and beautiful antiques and collectible Barbies. In winter, there is skiing only one hour away in the bordering mountains.

After a busy day, return to the inn and pamper yourself with an afternoon snack, where you can meet fellow guests, chat with your host, or just relax in the pleasant luxury of the two sitting rooms.

Macadamia Nut French Toast

Yield: 4 to 6 servings

1 (16-oz.) loaf Italian bread, cut into 1-inch-thick slices
4 large eggs, lightly beaten
¼ cup sugar
¼ tsp nutmeg plus extra, for garnish
⅔ cup orange juice
⅓ cup milk
½ tsp vanilla extract
1 stick plus 3 Tbsp butter or margarine, melted
½ cup chopped macadamia nuts
   Powdered sugar, for garnish
   Maple syrup, for serving

Plan ahead, this French toast needs to be started the night before.

Fit bread in a single layer in a lightly greased 9x13-inch baking pan. Mix eggs, sugar, nutmeg, orange juice, milk and vanilla; pour over bread. Cover and refrigerate overnight, turning bread once.

The next day, preheat oven to 400°F. Pour butter in a 15x10-inch jellyroll pan. Place bread in a single layer on top of butter. Bake for 10 minutes. Sprinkle with nuts and bake for 10 minutes more. Sprinkle with powdered sugar and nutmeg, if desired. Serve immediately with maple syrup.

THE WHITE DOE INN

INNKEEPERS	Bebe & Bob Woody
ADDRESS	319 Sir Walter Raleigh Street, Manteo, NC 27954
TELEPHONE	252-473-9851	800-473-6091
CONTACT	whitedoe@whitedoeinn.com	www.whitedoeinn.com
FEATURES	8 Rooms; Private baths	Children age 12 and older welcome	No pets, resident dog	Will accommodate guests' special dietary needs	Wireless Internet

The White Doe Inn harkens back to an era when guests were pampered, and the innkeepers make every effort to recapture that era of traveler comfort and camaraderie. Guest rooms and suites are distinctively decorated with family heirlooms and turn-of-the-century antiques. Rooms feature bedside gas-log fireplaces and several offer spa tubs for two.

The Inn is located on Roanoke Island, the perfect place to take advantage of all that this destination has to offer. Tucked in along the shores of Shallowbag Bay, the picturesque waterfront village of Manteo is surrounded by tranquil waters and is just minutes from Nags Head's beautiful beaches. Guests returning to the inn after a day of fun-filled adventure on the Outer Banks will find wonderful and delightful homemade desserts, a selection of Harney & Sons famous teas and delicious Green Mountain roasted coffee.

Raspberry Cream Cheese Coffee Cake

Yield: 1 Cake

"This is our signature coffee cake."—Innkeeper

2¼ cups all-purpose flour
1 cup sugar, divided
1½ sticks butter
½ tsp baking powder
½ tsp baking soda
1 tsp almond extract
¾ cup sour cream
3 eggs, divided
1 (8-oz.) pkg. cream cheese, softened
⅔ cup seedless raspberry preserves
½ cup sliced almonds

Preheat oven to 350°F. Grease and flour a 10-inch springform pan. In a large bowl, combine flour and ¾ cup of sugar. Cut in butter with a pastry blender or two knives until mixture is crumbly. Remove 1 cup of flour mixture and set aside for topping. Add baking powder, baking soda, almond extract, sour cream, and 1 egg to flour mixture in the large bowl; mix well and spread mixture over bottom and 2 inches up sides of pan.

Combine cream cheese, remaining ¼ cup of sugar and remaining 2 eggs; mix well and spoon over crust. Carefully spoon raspberry preserves over cream cheese mixture. Combine reserved 1 cup of flour mixture and almonds; sprinkle over preserves. Bake for 45–55 minutes. Cool for 15 minutes in pan, then remove sides of pan and cool cake completely.

THE YELLOW HOUSE

INNKEEPER	Shawn Bresnahan
ADDRESS	89 Oakview Drive, Waynesville, NC 28786
TELEPHONE	828-452-0991 | 800-563-1236
CONTACT	info@theyellowhouse.com | www.theyellowhouse.com
FEATURES	10 Rooms; Private baths | Children age 12 and older welcome | Will accommodate guests' special dietary needs

The Yellow House on Plott Creek Road is located just outside of Waynesville, in the country, at an elevation of 3,000 feet. The inn is 25 miles from Asheville, 10 minutes from the Blue Ridge Parkway and 20 minutes from the Great Smoky Mountain National Park. Nearby are Cataloochee Ski Area, Maggie Valley and the Pisgah National Forest.

At the Inn, you will enjoy the restful, relaxing and romantic mood of the Yellow House, as well as the mountain atmosphere of the Blue Ridge and Great Smoky Mountains of North Carolina. Each room offers a private bath, relaxing sitting area, gas-log fireplace, and refrigerator. Many have jetted tubs, a private patio or balcony, and wet bar. Thoughtful details abound: candles, plush terry-lined robes, herbal bath salts, piped-in music, and thick towels. The grounds and gardens are truly special and help to make your stay here unique. Our

five beautiful, rolling acres offer two stocked ponds, a stream, waterfall, walking paths, and many native plants for our guests to enjoy.

Outrageous French Toast

Yield: 8 servings

  1 cup packed light brown sugar
  1 Tbsp light Karo syrup
  5 Tbsp butter
  1 tsp cinnamon
 16 slices whole-wheat bread, crusts removed
  5 eggs
 1½ cups milk
  1 tsp vanilla extract
     Sour cream, for serving
     Fresh or frozen strawberries, for serving

Plan ahead, this French toast needs to be started the night before.

Grease a 9x13-inch baking pan. Combine brown sugar, Karo syrup, butter, and cinnamon in a small saucepan over low heat; cook, stirring, until sugar is melted and combined. Pour brown sugar mixture into baking pan and spread evenly. Top with 8 slices of bread, squeezing or cutting to fit if needed. Top with remaining bread, squeezing or cutting to fit if needed. Beat eggs, milk, and vanilla; pour over bread, cover and refrigerate overnight.

The next morning, preheat oven to 350°F. Bake French toast for 45 minutes. Cut into 8 pieces, then invert each serving onto a plate, sugar-side-up. Serve topped with a dollop of sour cream and strawberries.

Biscuits, Breads, Muffins & Scones

Inn at Bingham School
Biscuits

Yield: four 2½-inch biscuits

2 cups all-purpose flour
1 tsp salt
2 tsp sugar
1 Tbsp baking powder
1–1½ cups heavy cream (could substitute milk or buttermilk to lower calories)
5 Tbsp melted butter

Preheat oven to 425°F. In a bowl combine flour, salt, sugar, and baking powder. Slowly mix in cream until dough comes together. Turn dough out onto lightly floured countertop. The trick to biscuits is using a very light hand, which is why I prefer to use my hands rather than a rolling pin; too much kneading will lead to tough biscuits. With hands, flatten dough to about ½ inch thickness.

Using a 2½-inch round cookie cutter, cut into circles trying not to twist cutter as you lift, instead lift cutter straight up; the twisting motion will toughen biscuits. At this point you could wrap and freeze biscuits up to 1 month. (To bake frozen, simply take out of freezer and place directly on baking sheet increasing cooking time.) Dip biscuits to coat all sides in melted butter and place ½-inch apart on a parchment lined baking sheet. Placing biscuits closer together gives you softer edges which I prefer; if you like them browned, leave more space between biscuits. Bake in oven for 12 minutes, turn sheet and bake a few more minutes until lightly golden. Enjoy warm with cold butter and jam.

THE MOSS HOUSE B&B
Beckie's Banana Pecan Bread

Yield: Two 9x5 or 7 small loaves

*"Warm and spread with good butter and jam, you cannot beat this recipe.
It freezes beautifully and I make it often for guests and
gift giving, too!"*—Innkeeper

1	cup pecans	4	very ripe bananas
1½	cups sugar	4	eggs
4	cups all-purpose flour	⅔	cup plain yogurt
2	tsp baking soda	2	tsp vanilla
1	Tbsp salt	1	cup butter, melted
½–1	tsp cinnamon		and cooled
½	tsp grated nutmeg	¼	cup Turbinado sugar
½	tsp cardamom		

Preheat oven to 350°F and spray inside of pans with nonstick cooking spray. Toast 1 cup pecans for 5 minutes or until fragrant, allow to cool. In a bowl, mix next 7 ingredients and set aside. In another bowl, mash the bananas. In a third bowl, mix the remaining ingredients, except the Turbinado sugar, then add the mashed bananas. Mix wet ingredients into the flour mix and stir by hand until combined. Add most of the toasted pecans, chopped, and stir in. Do not over mix! Divide into pans and sprinkle with the Turbinado sugar. Bake for 40–55 minutes (check after 35 minutes) Test with toothpick.

These freeze very well. I reheat them with a little extra Turbinado sugar on top. My favorite variation: Fill pans with half the batter and drop bits of jam (raspberry is divine) down the center. Add the remaining batter on top and then sprinkle with sugar.

Inn at Iris Meadows B&B
Best Ever Banana Nut Bread

Yield: 1 loaf or 10–12 slices

"The baking aroma of this delicious bread is delightful!"—Innkeeper

1¾	cups all-purpose flour
1½	cup sugar
1	tsp baking soda
½	tsp salt
2	eggs
2	medium ripe bananas, mashed
½	cup vegetable oil
¼	cup plus 1 Tbsp buttermilk
1	tsp vanilla extract
1	cup chopped walnuts

Preheat oven to 325°F. In a large bowl, combine flour, sugar, baking soda, and salt. In another mixing bowl, combine eggs, bananas, oil, buttermilk, and vanilla; add to dry ingredients, stirring just until combined. Fold in nuts. Pour into a greased 9x5-inch loaf pan. Bake for one hour and 20 minutes or until a toothpick inserted near the center comes out clean. Cool for 10 minutes, then remove from pan to a wire rack.

Buffalo Tavern B&B

Buffalo Tavern Beer Bread

Yield: 1 loaf

"Easy, easy, easy and delicious!"—Innkeeper

3   cups self-rising flour
3   Tbsp sugar
1   can beer
3   Tbsp butter, melted

Preheat oven to 375°F. Spray oblong bread pan with baking spray (cooking spray that includes flour). Mix ingredients and pour into pan. Let rise for 15 minutes. Bake for 60 minutes. When done, brush some butter on top.

Self-rising flour is an all-purpose flour to which baking powder and salt have been added.

THE KING'S DAUGHTERS INN
English Muffin Bread

Yield: 2 loaves

2 cups milk
½ cup water
2 Tbsp cornmeal
6 cups bread flour, divided
2 (.25 oz.) pkgs. active dry yeast
1 Tbsp white sugar
2 tsp salt
¼ tsp baking soda

Warm the milk and water in a small saucepan until very warm (125°F). Lightly grease two 8x4-inch loaf pans; sprinkle cornmeal inside pans. In a large bowl, mix together 3 cups flour, yeast, sugar, salt, and soda. Stir milk into flour mixture; beat well. Stir in remaining flour, 1 cup at a time, until a stiff batter is formed. Spoon batter into prepared pans. Cover and let rise in a warm place until nearly doubled in size, about 45 minutes. Meanwhile, preheat oven to 400°F. Bake in preheated oven until golden brown, about 25 minutes. Remove from pans immediately and cool.

Fuquay Mineral Springs Inn
Foccacia Bread

Yield: 6–8 servings

2¾	cups all-purpose flour
1	tsp salt
1	tsp white sugar
1	Tbsp active dry yeast
1	tsp garlic powder
1	tsp dried oregano
1	tsp dried thyme
½	tsp dried basil
1	pinch ground black pepper
2	Tbsp olive oil
1	cup water
1	Tbsp grated Parmesan cheese
	sea salt

In a large bowl, stir together the flour, salt, sugar, yeast, garlic powder, oregano, thyme, basil, and black pepper. Mix in the olive oil and water. When the dough has pulled together, turn it out onto a lightly floured surface, and knead until smooth and elastic. Lightly oil a large bowl, place the dough in the bowl, and turn to coat with oil. Cover with a damp cloth and let rise in a warm place for 20 minutes.

Preheat oven to 450°F (230°C). Punch dough down; place on greased baking sheet. Pat into a ½-inch thick rectangle. Brush top with olive oil. Sprinkle with Parmesan cheese, herbs, and sea salt. Bake in preheated oven for 15 minutes, or until golden brown. Serve warm.

GLADE VALLEY B&B
Orange Cinnamon Bread

Yield: 2 loaves

2	Tbsp active dry yeast
¼	cup warm water (110°F to 115°F)
1	cup milk
¾	cup orange juice
1	cup sugar, divided
1	Tbsp grated orange peel
1½	tsp salt
1	egg
6½ to 7	cups bread flour, divided
2	tsp ground cinnamon

In a large mixing bowl, dissolve yeast in warm water. In a saucepan, heat milk and orange juice to 110°F; add to yeast mixture. Stir in ½ cup sugar, orange peel, salt, egg and 3 cups of flour; beat until smooth. Stir in enough remaining flour to form a soft dough.

Turn onto a floured surface; knead until smooth and elastic, about 6 to 8 minutes. Place in a greased bowl, turning once to grease top. Cover and let rise in a warm place until doubled, about 1 hour.

Punch dough down. Turn onto a lightly floured surface; divide in half. Roll each portion into a 15x7-inch rectangle. Brush with water. Combine cinnamon and remaining sugar; sprinkle over dough to within 1 inch of edges. Tightly roll up jelly-roll style, starting with a short side; pinch seams to seal. Place seam-side down in two greased 9x5x3-inch loaf pans. Cover and let rise until doubled, about 1 hour.

Bake at 350°F for 35–40 minutes or until golden brown. Remove from pans and place on wire racks to cool.

AppleWood Manor Inn B&B
Pumpkin Blooper Bread

Yield: 2 loaves or 12 servings

"This is actually a mistake that turned out to be heaven. It is another guest favorite which we serve toasted with cream cheese on the side. Stores well double-wrapped in plastic wrap for up to a week. Actually best served after refrigeration for 24 hours."—Innkeeper

- 1½ cups canola oil
- 4 eggs
- 3 cups sugar
- 3 cups flour
- 2 tsp baking powder
- 2 tsp baking soda
- 3 tsp cinnamon
- 1 (30-oz.) can Libby's Pumpkin Pie mix
- 2 cups finely chopped toasted pecans
- 1 tsp real vanilla

Preheat oven to 350°F. Spray two 9-inch loaf pans. Beat oil, eggs and sugar with mixer. In a separate bowl, with a wire wisk combine flour, baking powder, baking soda and cinnamon, and mix well. Alternate adding pumpkin pie mix and flour mixture to the egg mixture, beating softly after each addition. Add toasted pecans and vanilla, fold into pumpkin/flour mixture. This will be very thin batter. Divide evenly between both pans. Bake 1 hour and 20 minutes. If using a convection oven, reduce temperature to 325 and bake for 1 hour 15 minutes. Remove from pan when completely cooled.

Inn on Main Street
Whole Grain Bread

Yield: 1 loaf

"This basic bread goes with egg dishes for breakfast, but also is the basis for our baked apple French toast (see page 140). We also make the dough into baguettes for bruschetta, and add herbs and feta to make focaccia. We use an old coffee grinder to grind flax seeds."—Innkeeper

1	cup warm water
¼	cup honey
2	Tbsp yeast
1	cup white bread flour
1	tsp salt
¼	cup canola oil
¼	cup ground flax seeds
1	cup whole-wheat flour
¼	cup wheat bran

Preheat oven to 350°F. Mix water, honey and yeast. Microwave white flour a minute. While waiting, mix salt, oil, and flax meal into the liquid mixture. Add heated white flour and mix in, then add whole-wheat flour and bran, kneading dough thoroughly. If mixture seems too dry, add a bit more warm water. If too wet, sprinkle on white bread flour as needed. Allow dough to rise twice for about an hour each time, beating it down after each rising.

Spray a bread pan with oil, shape and insert loaf, and allow to rise for a half hour. Slit the top to allow expansion, then bake for 45 minutes. Dough may be stored in a plastic storage bag in the fridge for up to five days before baking.

BROOKSIDE MOUNTAIN MIST INN B&B

Bran Muffins

Yield: 12–14 muffins

1	cup shreds of Whole Bran cereal
1¼	cups buttermilk
¼	cup vegetable oil
1	egg
1¼	cup flour
¾	cup sugar
¾	tsp baking soda
½	tsp baking powder
¼	tsp salt
½	cup raisins

Preheat oven to 400°F. In a large bowl, combine cereal and buttermilk, stir well. Let stand for 5 minutes until cereal is softened. Add oil and egg, mix well with a hand mixer. Add remaining ingredients, mix well. Fill muffin tins with liners ¾ full. Bake for 18–20 minutes or until toothpick inserted in center comes out clean. Serve warm.

Note: This batter can be baked immediately or stored in tightly covered container in the refrigerator for up to 2 weeks.

The Inn on Mill Creek
Chocolate Chip Banana Muffins
Yield: 10–12 muffins

1 stick (8 Tbsp) butter or margarine, softened to room temperature
1 cup sugar
2 eggs
3 ripe bananas
1 Tbsp milk
1 tsp cinnamon
2 cups flour, sifted
1 tsp baking powder
1 tsp baking soda
½ tsp salt
½ cup chocolate chips (chocoholics can add up to 1 cup …
your choice!)

Preheat oven to 350°F. In a mixing bowl, mix the butter and sugar well, then add eggs one at a time. In a medium bowl, combine bananas and milk. We find a fork works best to mash the bananas. Mix in the cinnamon until blended. In another bowl, combine sifted flour, baking powder, baking soda, and salt. Add bananas to the butter/sugar/egg mixture, then add flour mixture until batter forms. Add chocolate chips. Spoon into greased muffin pans and bake for 30 minutes. Serve warm or allow to cool—either way they're good!

Note: We also make these muffins gluten free using King Arthur Gluten Free Flour with 1 tsp of xantham gum for every cup of flour.

OLD NORTH DURHAM INN
Creamy Corn Muffins

Yield: 10–12 muffins

1 (8.5-oz.) box corn muffin mix
1 (8.5-oz.) can cream style corn
1 egg
2 heaping Tbsp sour cream

Preheat oven to 400°F. In a bowl, mix all ingredients together. Spray the muffin cups with cooking spray. Fill cups about ½ full. Bake about 15–20 minutes or until golden brown.

Before settlers came to the New World, Europeans had never seen corn. What a wonderfully versatile and useful gift the Indians gave the world.

Inn on Main Street
Gluten-Free Muffins

Yield: 12 muffins

"This is our generic muffin recipe, simply substituting brown rice flour for wheat flour. Get brown rice flour at any health food store. It makes a more crumbly muffin than conventional flour, but tastes great." —Innkeeper

- 1 cup sugar
- 1 tsp salt
- 1 tsp baking soda
- 1 tsp baking powder
- 1 tsp pure vanilla
- ½ tsp ground nutmeg
- ½ cup fruit (berries, applesauce, chopped mango, mashed bananas, etc.)
- ½ cup canola oil
- 1 egg
- 1 cup buttermilk
- 2 cups brown rice flour

Preheat oven to 350°F. In a bowl, mix sugar, salt, baking soda and baking powder, spices, and fruit. Beat in oil, egg, and buttermilk. Mix in rice flour until everything is just blended—do not over mix. Spoon batter into muffin tins sprayed with vegetable oil. Bake for 40 minutes, or until tops are brown.

803 Elizabeth B&B

Low-Fat Applesauce Muffin Tops

Yield: 12 muffin tops or 8 regular muffins

"This recipe is adapted from the book Innkeepers' Best Muffins *by Laura Zahn. The low-fat content makes them heavier than usual muffins, but try them, you'll like them!"*—Innkeeper

- 1¼ cups applesauce
- 1 tsp vanilla extract
- 1½ cups unbleached all-purpose flour
- ½ cup whole-wheat flour
- ½ cup plus 1 Tbsp sugar, divided
- 1½ tsp baking powder
- 1 tsp baking soda
- 1 tsp cinnamon
- ½ cup chopped nuts
- ½ cup Craisins or dried cranberries
- ½ tsp nutmeg

Preheat oven to 350°F. In a large bowl, combine applesauce and vanilla. In a medium bowl, combine all-purpose and whole-wheat flours, ½ cup of sugar, baking powder, baking soda, and cinnamon. Add flour mixture to applesauce mixture and stir just to combine (do not over mix). Stir in nuts and Craisins.

Spoon batter (or use an ice cream scoop) into greased or paper-lined muffin top or regular muffin cups. Combine nutmeg and remaining 1 tablespoon of sugar; sprinkle about ¼ teaspoon of nutmeg mixture over batter in each muffin cup. Bake for 20–25 minutes.

INN ON MAIN STREET
Sweet Potato Muffins

Yield: 12 muffins

"This is our most requested recipe. Substitute mashed pumpkin for sweet potato to get a similar muffin. These muffins are denser and chewier than you normally expect in a muffin."—Innkeeper

1	cup brown sugar
1	cup freshly grated or mashed sweet potatoes
1	tsp unsulfured molasses
1	tsp pure vanilla
1	tsp ground ginger
½	tsp ground nutmeg
½	tsp ground cloves
1	tsp baking powder
1	tsp baking soda
1	tsp salt
½	cup canola oil
1	egg
1	cup buttermilk
2	cups white unbleached all-purpose flour

Preheat oven to 350°F. Mix brown sugar, sweet potatoes, molasses, vanilla, and dry ingredients except flour. Mix in oil, egg, and buttermilk. Add flour and mix as little as possible to blend ingredients. Spoon batter into muffin tins sprayed with vegetable oil. Bake for 40 minutes or until tops brown.

Glade Valley B&B
Cranberry Orange Scones

Yield: 10 scones

2 cups all-purpose flour
10 tsp sugar, divided
1 Tbsp grated orange peel
2 tsp baking powder
½ tsp salt
¼ tsp baking soda
⅓ cup cold butter
1 cup dried cranberries
¼ cup orange juice
¼ cup half & half cream
1 egg
1 Tbsp milk

Glaze:

½ cup confectioners' sugar
1 Tbsp orange juice

Preheat oven to 400°F. In a bowl, combine flour, 7 teaspoons sugar, orange peel, baking powder, salt, and baking soda. Cut in butter until the mixture resembles coarse crumbs; set aside. In a small bowl, combine cranberries, orange juice, cream, and egg. Add to flour mixture and stir until a soft dough forms. Turn out onto a floured surface; gently knead 6–8 times. Pat dough into an 8-inch circle. Cut into 10 wedges. Separate wedges and place on a ungreased baking sheet. Brush with milk and sprinkle with remaining 3 teaspoons sugar. Bake for 12 minutes or until lightly browned, then remove from oven. Combine glaze ingredients; drizzle over scones.

Hill House B&B
Cranberry Orange Scones

Yield: 16 scones

2 cups flour
2 Tbsp sugar
2 Tbsp baking powder
1 tsp salt
6 Tbsp butter, cold
1 Tbsp finely grated orange zest
1 cup dried cranberries
1 egg, beaten
½ cup milk

Glaze:

½ cup powdered sugar
2 Tbsp orange juice
1 tsp orange zest

Preheat oven to 350°F. In large bowl combine flour, sugar, baking powder, and salt. Cut the butter into the flour until mixture looks like fine crumbs. Stir in orange zest and dried cranberries. Add egg and milk and stir together until mixture forms a soft dough. Turn dough onto lightly floured surface and knead gently, about 15 times. Divide dough in half and pat into two circles, ½-inch thick. Cut each circle into 8 wedges and place each on a lightly greased baking sheet. Bake about 15 minutes until very lightly browned.

While the scones are baking, make the glaze. Mix powdered sugar, orange juice, and orange zest until combined. Brush glaze over hot scones and enjoy!

Inn at Bingham School
Cranberry Pecan Scones

Yield: 6 scones

- 1¾ cups all-purpose flour
- 1 Tbsp plus ½ tsp baking powder
- ¼ cup plus 2 Tbsp sugar
- ½ tsp kosher salt
- 6 Tbsp chilled unsalted butter, diced in small pieces
- ¼ cup pecan pieces
- ¼ cup dried cranberries
- 1 cup plus 2 Tbsp heavy cream, divided
- 1 Tbsp Demerara sugar

In the bowl of an electric mixer with a paddle attachment, combine flour, baking powder, sugar and salt. Add the butter and place bowl in freezer for 5 minutes. Afterwards, beat the mixture on low speed for 3 minutes, butter should be broken into pebble-size pieces. Add pecans and dried cranberries. With mixer on low, add 1 cup of cream and mix just until dough comes together. Turn dough out onto lightly floured counter. With your hands, shape into a 7-inch circle. Cut the dough into 6 wedges. Freeze the scones for an hour or wrapped up to a month.

Preheat oven to 375°F. Line baking sheet with parchment paper. I usually put an additional baking pan underneath to keep the bottoms from browning too much. Place scones on parchment about ½-inch apart. Brush tops with cream and sprinkle with Demerara sugar. Bake for 15 minutes, turn baking sheet and bake another 10 minutes, until edges are brown and tops light golden.

Carol's Garden Inn
Oatmeal Scones

Yield: 8 scones

1½ cups rolled or quick oats
¼ cup whole milk
¼ cup heavy cream
1 egg
1½ cups flour
⅓ cup sugar, plus 1 Tbsp for sprinkling
2 tsp baking powder
½ tsp salt
10 Tbsp cold unsalted butter, cut into ½-inch cubes

Preheat oven to 375°F and adjust oven rack to middle position. Spread oats evenly on baking sheet and toast until lightly browned, 7–8 minutes. Set aside to cool. When oats are cool, measure out 2 tablespoons and set aside. Whisk milk, cream, and egg until incorporated. Remove 1 tablespoon to a small bowl and reserve for glazing. Pulse flour, ⅓-cup sugar, baking powder, and salt in food processor until combined. Scatter butter evenly over dry ingredients and pulse until mixture resembles cornmeal. Transfer to a medium bowl. Stir in oats and liquid ingredients until large clumps form. Mix dough by hand until dough forms a ball.

Dust work surface with 1 tablespoon reserved oats. Turn dough over and dust the top with remaining 1 tablespoon of oats. Gently pat into a 7-inch circle about 1 inch thick. Cut dough into 8 wedges. Brush surfaces with reserved egg mixture and sprinkle with 1 tablespoon sugar. Bake until golden brown, about 12–14 minutes. Cool for 5 minutes on baking sheet on wire rack. Then remove from baking sheet and serve.

French Toast, Pancakes & Waffles

BROOKSIDE MOUNTAIN MIST INN B&B

Banana-Nut French Toast

Yield: 8–10 servings

6 Tbsp butter, melted
1½ cups packed brown sugar
5 large ripe bananas, cut diagonally into ½-inch thick slices
1 loaf French bread, cut into 1-inch thick slices
6 eggs
2 cups milk
2 tsp vanilla
1 tsp ground cinnamon
½ cup pecans or walnuts

Plan ahead—this recipe requires overnight refrigeration.

In a bowl, mix butter and brown sugar by hand until well moistened. With fingertips, press sugar mixture onto bottom of a 9x13-inch baking dish; mixture may not cover the entire bottom of dish. Spread banana over mixture. Place bread slices on top of bananas. In a bowl, whisk together eggs, milk, vanilla, and cinnamon. Slowly pour milk mixture over bread, pressing bread down to absorb liquid. Sprinkle nuts on top. Cover and refrigerate overnight. In the morning, preheat oven to 350°F. Bake uncovered for 50–55 minutes or until bread is golden brown. Let stand 10 minutes before serving.

Inn on Main Street
Nancy's Baked Apple French Toast

Yield: 2 servings

*"There are several variations on this recipe involving different fruit, but
Nancy made it healthier and local by decreasing the amount of butter, using our whole-grain homemade bread (see page 127), and increasing the
amount of North Carolina apples."*—Innkeeper

2 eggs
¼ cup buttermilk
    dash of pure vanilla
¼ tsp salt
2 slices whole-grain bread, with hard crusts removed
1 pat butter
1 tsp brown sugar
1 large Granny Smith apple, peeled, cored, and sliced
1 oz. cream cheese
¼ tsp cinnamon

Preheat oven 350°F. Mix eggs, buttermilk, vanilla, and salt. Add bread
and allow to soak several minutes. (You can soak it overnight if
you'd like to prepare it in advance). Melt butter in a skillet over medium heat. Mix in brown sugar, then add and coat apple slices. Allow
to sauté until slightly cooked. Place apples in a small casserole dish
sprayed with vegetable oil. Flatten dollops of cream cheese and lay
them on top of apples as evenly as possible. Place bread over apples,
then pour remaining egg mixture over bread. Punch holes in bread
with a chopstick or fingers if necessary to allow extra mixture to
seep into layer of apples as well. Sprinkle top of dish with cinnamon.
Bake for 45 minutes. Serve with maple syrup, if desired.

Carol's Garden Inn
Orange French Toast

Yield: 4 servings

4	eggs
⅔	cup orange juice
⅓	cup milk
¼–½	cup amaretto
½	cup sugar
½	tsp vanilla
¼	tsp nutmeg
8	thick slices French bread

Plan ahead—needs overnight refrigeration.

Mix all ingredients (except bread) together in a large bowl. In a large pan arrange bread in a single layer and top with egg mixture. Refrigerate overnight. Grill and serve with Orange Marmalade syrup.

Orange Marmalade Syrup

In a small saucepan, heat orange marmalade with a little orange juice and amaretto.

ANDON-REID INN B&B

Orange-Pecan French Toast

Yield: 6–8 servings

  1 cup packed brown sugar
⅓ cup melted butter
  2 Tbsp light colored corn syrup
⅓ cup chopped pecans
  2 tsp grated orange rind
  1 cup orange juice
½ cup skim milk
  3 Tbsp sugar
  1 tsp cinnamon
  1 tsp vanilla extract
  5 large eggs
12 (1-inch thick) slices French bread

Plan ahead—needs overnight refrigeration.

In a bowl, combine brown sugar, melted butter, and corn syrup; pour into a 13x9-inch pan coated with cooking spray. Sprinkle chopped pecans evenly over sugar mixture. Combine rind and next 6 ingredients (rind through eggs), stir with a whisk. Arrange bread slices over pecans in pan, pour egg mixture over bread. Cover and refrigerate overnight.

Preheat oven to 350°F. Carefully turn bread slices over to absorb excess egg mixture. Let stand at room temperature for 20 minutes. Bake for 35 minutes or until lightly browned.

THE YELLOW HOUSE
Outrageous French Toast

Yield: 8 servings

     1 cup packed light brown sugar
     1 Tbsp light Karo syrup
     5 Tbsp butter
     1 tsp cinnamon
    16 slices whole-wheat bread, crusts removed
     5 eggs
    1½ cups milk
     1 tsp vanilla extract
       Sour cream, for serving
       Fresh or frozen strawberries, for serving

Plan ahead, this French toast needs to be started the night before.

Grease a 9x13-inch baking pan. Combine brown sugar, Karo syrup, butter, and cinnamon in a small saucepan over low heat; cook, stirring, until sugar is melted and combined. Pour brown sugar mixture into baking pan and spread evenly. Top with 8 slices of bread, squeezing or cutting to fit, if needed. Top with remaining bread, squeezing or cutting to fit, if needed. Beat eggs, milk, and vanilla; pour over bread, cover and refrigerate overnight.

The next morning, preheat oven to 350°F. Bake French toast for 45 minutes. Cut into 8 pieces, then invert each serving onto a plate, sugar-side-up. Serve topped with a dollop of sour cream and strawberries.

Glade Valley B&B

Oven Pecan French Toast

Yield: 6–8 servings

1½ sticks unsalted butter
1 cup light brown sugar
1 cup coarsely chopped pecans
8 eggs
1½ cups milk
1 tsp vanilla
Few dashes cinnamon
1 loaf French bread, sliced 1-inch thick

Preheat oven to 350°F. Place butter sticks in a 10x15-inch pan and place in oven until just melted. Remove from oven and stir in sugar, distributing resulting syrup evenly over bottom of pan. Sprinkle with pecans. In a bowl, beat the eggs, milk, vanilla, and cinnamon. Dip bread slices one at a time into mix and place slices on top of syrup in pan. Pour remaining egg mixture over the slices. Bake for 35–40 minutes, or until golden brown.

803 Elizabeth B&B
Overnight French Toast

Yield: 6–8 servings

Spray 3-quart dish with cooking spray. Cut a French bread loaf into 1-inch slices and place in dish.

In a bowl, mix together:

6 eggs
1½ cups half & half
1½ cups milk
1 tsp vanilla
1 tsp cinnamon
½ tsp nutmeg

Pour over bread and cover. Place in refrigerator overnight.

Topping

½ cup butter
½ cup brown sugar
½ cup oatmeal
½ cup flour
½ cup of chopped nuts

In a bowl, mix together butter, sugar, oatmeal and flour until crumbly and then add nuts.

In the morning preheat oven to 350°F. Crumble the topping over the bread and bake for about 40 minutes.

Note: I use the topping on everything from a cobbler to muffins. You can adjust the quantity to whatever amount you need. Just mix equal quantities of the five ingredients. Cinnamon and nutmeg can also be added.

Inn at Iris Meadows B&B
Truly Decadent Stuffed French Toast with Warm Apricot Syrup

Yield: 6 servings

"A popular dish with all of our guests! The hint of ginger distinguishes this toast from all the others." —Innkeeper

- 1 (8-oz.) pkg. cream cheese, softened
- ¼ cup crushed pineapple
- ½ cup chopped pecans, toasted
- 1 (16-oz.) loaf French bread (Italian bread works even better since it is dense enough to hold together upon stuffing)

- 4 large eggs
- 1 cup whipping cream
- ½ tsp vanilla extract
- 1 tsp ground ginger

- 1 (12-oz.) jar apricot preserves
- ½ cup orange juice

Beat cream cheese and pineapple at medium speed in an electric mixer until light and fluffy; stir in chopped toasted pecans. Cut bread into 12 (1½-inch thick) slices; cut a pocket through top crust of each slice. Stuff each slice evenly with cream cheese mixture. In a bowl, combine eggs and next 3 ingredients, stirring well with a wire whisk.

Dip bread slices in egg mixture, coating all sides. Cook on a lightly greased griddle over medium-high heat—3 minutes on each side or until golden. Stand the pieces up to brown the top and bottom edges. Combine preserves and orange juice in a saucepan. Cook over low heat, stirring constantly, until melted. Serve over hot toast.

Top with fresh whipped cream and sliced strawberries and blueberries. Garnish with fresh mint sprigs.

OAKLAND COTTAGE B&B
Vegan Fruity Baked French Toast

Yield: 6 servings

- 1 cup sliced peaches or other fruit
- 1–2 Tbsp apple juice and/or maple syrup
- 6 slices of vegan bread, ¾-inch thick (or enough to cover bottom of baking dish)
- 5 egg substitutes, I use a mixture of:
  1 substitute = ¼ cup mashed banana (I like to use a thawed-out frozen banana)
  1 substitute = ¼ cup applesauce
  3 substitutes = 6 Tbsp water plus 3 Tbsp canola or olive oil plus 1½ tsp baking powder
- 1½ cups soy milk (or any milk substitute)
- 1 Tbsp vanilla extract
  Cinnamon

Plan ahead—dish needs overnight refrigeration.

Grease a 13x9x2-inch baking dish. Mix peaches and apple juice and place in the bottom of the baking dish. Arrange vegan bread in any way over the peaches, covering the bottom of the baking dish. In a bowl, whisk the egg substitutes, soy milk, and vanilla. Slowly pour the mixture over the bread, then sprinkle with cinnamon. Cover with aluminum foil and refrigerate for 8 hours or overnight.

Remove from the fridge for 30 minutes or more before baking. Preheat oven to 350°F. Bake covered for 30 minutes, then remove foil and bake for 30 more minutes, or until firm in the center and golden brown. Cool for 15 minutes before cutting. Arrange on a serving dish with fresh fruit garnish. Serve with dairy-free yogurt substitute (coconut or soy).

OLD NORTH DURHAM INN
Banana Pancakes

Yield: 8 4-inch pancakes

"This is a basic pancake recipe in which any fruit can be used. This banana version is a favorite of our guests, very sweet and light. It is also great without fruit."—Innkeeper

1 cup sifted all-purpose flour
2 tsp baking powder
½ tsp salt
2 Tbsp sugar
1 egg
1 cup milk
3 Tbsp melted butter
2 ripe bananas, sliced

Heat griddle or heavy skillet. Grease griddle (we use margarine). Griddle is ready when a sprinkle of cold water rolls off in drops.

Sift dry ingredients in a small bowl. Beat egg, milk and melted butter in a separate bowl until well mixed. Add dry ingredients to wet ingredients. Stir until combined (batter will be lumpy). The secret to the fluffiness in these and all pancakes is to keep the wet and dry ingredients separate until the griddle is ready for cooking.

Drop ¼-cup batter onto griddle for each pancake. Place 5 slices of banana on top of each. Cook until bubbles form on top of each pancake and edges become dry. Flip and cook for about 2 minutes or until pancake is nicely browned on underside.

Inn at Iris Meadows B&B
Classic Buttermilk Pancakes with Caramelized Bananas

Yield: about 14 four-inch pancakes (4 servings)

2 cups all-purpose flour
2 tsp sugar
1 tsp baking powder
1 tsp baking soda
¼ tsp salt
2 large eggs, separated

2 cups plus 2 Tbsp buttermilk
2 Tbsp unsalted butter, melted, or canola oil, plus extra for greasing

Combine flour, sugar, baking powder, baking soda, and salt in a large bowl. In a small, deep bowl, beat the egg whites with an electric mixer until soft, glossy peaks form. In another bowl, beat or whisk together the egg yolks, buttermilk, and butter. Add the buttermilk mixture to the dry ingredients; mix just until combined. Fold in the egg whites.

Heat a griddle or large skillet over medium heat and grease lightly. For each pancake, spoon or pour about ¼ cup batter onto the hot griddle. Cook until bubbles appear on the surface and the edges look dry, about 2 minutes. Turn over and cook until golden brown, about 1 minute more.

Serve with butter and maple syrup, or caramelized bananas and a dollop of whipped cream.

Caramelized Bananas

3½ oz. butter
3 Tbsp dark corn syrup
3 large ripe bananas, peeled and thickly sliced

Melt the butter with the corn syrup in a saucepan over low heat and stir until combined. Simmer for a few minutes until the caramel thickens and darkens slightly. Add the bananas and mix gently to coat. Pour over the warm pancakes and serve immediately.

Hill House B&B
German Puff Pancake

Yield: 4 servings

2 cups flour
1/8 tsp salt
2 cups milk
8 eggs
4 Tbsp melted butter
1/3 cup brown sugar
4 Granny Smith apples, sliced
cinnamon

Preheat oven 400°F. Mix together flour and salt in a small bowl. In a large bowl, blend milk and eggs. Add the flour and salt and mix well. Cover the bottom of a greased, 9x11-inch glass baking dish with melted butter. Sprinkle entire dish with brown sugar, then top with a layer of sliced apples. Sprinkle with desired amount of cinnamon and top with batter. Baked for 35 minutes. Remove from oven and immediately turn upside down on cutting board to remove pancake. Slice and serve with whipped cream and fresh fruit.

Inn at Bingham School
Basic Pancake Recipe

Yield: 4 servings

"This is the tastiest basic pancake recipe making room for whatever additions your heart desires. My boys always choose to add mini chocolate chips, my husband prefers blueberries and I love them simply with good maple syrup."—Innkeeper

1   cup all-purpose flour
1   tsp baking powder
½   tsp salt
1   egg
1   cup low-fat milk
½   tsp vanilla extract (Madagascar makes a difference)

Heat griddle over medium heat. In a mixing bowl, combine flour, baking powder, and salt. Whisk in egg, milk and vanilla extract. Mix just until combined, a few lumps are fine. Coat hot griddle with butter and ladle mixture onto griddle in shapes and sizes you prefer. Flip pancakes when you see bubbles in the middle. Enjoy!

A Bed of Roses, Victorian B&B

Peaches with Orange Sauce in a Puff Pancake

Yield: 4 servings (can easily be doubled)

Peaches with Orange Sauce:

- 2 Tbsp butter
- 2 tsp cornstarch
- 2 Tbsp sugar
- 5–6 peeled and sliced fresh peaches, or 1 bag of frozen peaches (don't use canned peaches!)
- 2 Tbsp orange juice
- 1 tsp vanilla

Puff Pancake:

- 4 eggs
- 1 cup milk
- 1 cup flour
  heavy dash of nutmeg

For the Sauce:

Place butter, corn starch, and sugar in a large nonstick saucepan along with peaches and sauté for 10 minutes until warmed through. Add orange juice and vanilla and simmer for 5 minutes.

For the Pancake:

Preheat oven to 425°F. Spray 4 Texas muffin tins or ramekins of the same size with nonstick cooking spray. Wisk the eggs, milk, flour, and nutmeg together and pour into the prepared tins so that each is $2/3$ to $3/4$ full. Bake for 25 minutes and watch the magic! They will deflate a little bit when they come out of the oven, but a natural hole will have formed in the middle of the "puff."

Assemble:

Dust pancakes with confectioners' sugar and place on individual plates. Pour warm peaches in orange sauce over the puffs, filling the hole and spilling over onto the plate. Garnish with an orange slice and a fanned strawberry.

THE KING'S DAUGHTERS INN
Pumpkin Pancakes

Yield: 12 servings

2	cups flour
¼	cup sugar
2¼	tsp baking powder
½	tsp baking soda
½	tsp salt
½	tsp pumpkin pie spice
2	eggs
1½	cups buttermilk
½	cup puréed pumpkin
¼	cup unsalted butter, melted

In a large bowl, mix together dry ingredients. In a separate bowl, mix together wet ingredients. Combine wet and dry ingredients until a lumpy batter is formed.

Be careful not to over mix!

Over medium heat, spoon ⅓ cup of batter onto a hot skillet for each pancake. Cook 2–3 minutes on each side.

Inn at Iris Meadows B&B
Oatmeal Belgian Waffles

Yield: 8 (5-inch) square waffles

*"We have tested many waffle recipes—this one wins
guest praises every time!"*—Innkeeper

1½ cups flour
1 cup quick-cooking rolled oats
1 Tbsp baking powder
½ tsp cinnamon
¼ tsp salt
2 eggs, slightly beaten
1½ cups milk
6 Tbsp butter, melted
2 Tbsp brown sugar

In a large bowl, mix together the flour, oats, baking powder, cinnamon, and salt. In small bowl, mix together eggs, milk, butter, and brown sugar. Add to flour mixture, and stir until blended. Cook according to your Belgian waffle maker instructions.

Serve with fresh whipped cream, topped with berries and real maple syrup.

Breakfast Entrées

THE YELLOW HOUSE
Autumn Vegetable Frittata

Yield: 6 servings

"This frittata can be prepared the night before and baked in the morning. You can substitute any vegetables you would like, such as broccoli, green or red bell peppers, celery, etc. Don't be afraid to experiment."—Innkeeper

3 links Italian sausage	3 large cloves garlic, minced
1 Tbsp vegetable oil	
2 small yellow squash, sliced	1 cup grated Parmesan cheese
1 large zucchini, sliced	½ tsp dried basil
1 large carrot, sliced	¼ tsp dried marjoram
1 medium onion, chopped	Salt and black pepper, to taste
6 oz. fresh mushrooms, sliced	1 cup grated cheese (cheddar, Swiss or a mixture)
6 eggs	

Preheat oven to 350°F. Remove sausages from casings and cook in a large skillet over medium heat, breaking up sausage into small pieces, until cooked through; drain on paper towels and set aside. Heat oil in a skillet over medium heat. Add squash, zucchini, carrot, onion, and mushrooms; cook until vegetables are crisp-tender.

In a large bowl, beat eggs, garlic, Parmesan cheese, basil, marjoram, salt, and pepper. Stir in sausage and vegetable mixture; pour mixture into a greased deep-dish pie pan or a 9x9-inch baking dish. Sprinkle with grated cheese. Bake for 30 minutes (or cover and refrigerate overnight and bake the next day).

Note: This frittata freezes well after it is baked. Thaw in the refrigerator, then heat through in a preheated 300°F, oven (don't overcook).

1889 WhiteGate Inn & Cottage
Bacon & Potato Strata

Yield: 8–12 servings

"This strata may be prepared the night before, covered, refrigerated and baked in the morning." —Innkeeper

 3 Tbsp vegetable oil
 ½ (26-oz.) pkg. frozen hash brown potatoes
 1 (3-oz.) pkg. Ready Crisp bacon bits or 3 oz. bacon, cooked and crumbled
 8 slices Canadian bacon, diced
 8 oz. mushrooms, sliced
 1 leek, chopped
16 eggs
1½ cups milk
 ½ tsp salt
 ½ tsp dried rosemary
 ¼ tsp dried thyme
 2 cups grated mozzarella cheese

Preheat oven to 350°F. Grease a 9x13-inch baking dish. Heat oil in a skillet over medium-high heat. Add hash browns and cook until soft. Layer hash browns, bacon bits, Canadian bacon, mushrooms, leeks, and cheese in baking dish.

Beat eggs, milk, salt, rosemary, and thyme, then pour over ingredients in baking dish. Bake for 1 hour, or until golden brown. Remove from oven and let stand for 5 minutes, then slice and serve.

BUFFALO TAVERN B&B
Stuffed Croissants

Yield: 12 sandwiches

12 croissants (from the grocery store)
12 slices Canadian bacon
4–5 Granny Smith apples, sliced
6 slices Monterrey Jack cheese (or your favorite), cut in half
4 eggs
2 cups milk
Nutmeg to taste
Cinnamon to taste

Preheat oven to 375°F. Slice croissants in half. Peel and slice apples and put on a large plate. Place the Canadian bacon on the plate along with the 12 slices of cheese. In a bowl, mix the eggs, milk, nutmeg, and cinnamon like making French toast mixture. Dip the bottom of each croissant in the mixture. On each croissant place apple slices, Canadian bacon, and a slice of cheese. Dip the top half in the egg/milk mixture and place the croissant on a well-sprayed baking sheet. Repeat with each croissant. Bake for 20–35 minutes. Serve with fruit.

Pamlico House B&B
Cheese Grits Casserole

Yield: 6–8 servings

1½	cups water
½	cup grits
2	eggs well beaten
¾	cup milk
	salt & pepper to taste
1	cup grated sharp cheddar cheese

Preheat oven to 325°F. Prepare grits according to directions. When thickened, remove from heat and add eggs, milk, and salt and pepper. Beat into grits and return to heat. Add cheese and stir until dissolved. Pour mixture into buttered 1-quart casserole (mixture will be like sauce). Bake for 1 hour or until soufflé consistency, serve hot. Recipe can be doubled or tripled. Great served with quiche.

"Grits" originally used to mean "hominy grits," but now applies to any coarsely ground grain such as corn, oats, or rice.

Glade Valley B&B
Cheese Grits Soufflé

Yield: 6 servings

2 cups water
½ cups grits
4 Tbsp butter
¾ cup shredded cheddar cheese
¼ tsp salt
2 large eggs
⅓ cup milk
¼ cup grated Parmesan cheese
pinch of paprika

Preheat oven to 350°F. Grease a round glass or ceramic baking dish or 6 ramekins. In a 2-quart saucepan, heat water to boiling. Reduce heat and whisk in the grits gradually. Reduce heat to low and cover. Cook 10–15 minutes until creamy and the water is absorbed. Transfer grits to a large bowl and add the butter, cheddar cheese, and salt. In a separate bowl, whisk the eggs and milk together, then add to the grits. Pour into the prepared dish. Sprinkle with cheese and paprika. Bake uncovered, 45–60 minutes (30 minutes for ramekins) until the top is golden and toothpick comes out clean.

THE YELLOW HOUSE
Chili Cheese Egg Puff

Yield: 8 servings

- 5 eggs, beaten well
- ¼ cup all-purpose flour
- 1 tsp salt
- 1 tsp baking powder
- 1 cup cottage cheese
- ½ stick butter, melted
- 1 (4-oz.) can chopped mild green chilies
- 2 cups grated colby cheese, divided
- 2 cups grated Monterey Jack cheese, divided

Preheat oven to 350°F. Grease a 7x9-inch glass baking dish. Combine eggs, flour, salt, baking powder, cottage cheese, butter, green chilies, 1 cup of colby cheese, and 1 cup of Monterey Jack cheese. Pour mixture into baking dish. Sprinkle with remaining cheeses and bake for 30–45 minutes, until cheese has melted.

1889 WhiteGate Inn & Cottage

Crab & Artichoke Egg Puff with White Wine Sauce

Yield: 4 servings

Egg puff:

- 5 eggs, beaten
- ¼ cup all-purpose flour
- ½ tsp baking powder
- 1 (8-oz.) carton cottage cheese
- 2 cups grated Monterey Jack cheese
- ¼ lb. shredded crabmeat (or imitation crabmeat)
- 6 oz. chopped artichoke hearts (not marinated)
  Salt and black pepper, to taste

White wine sauce:

- 2 Tbsp butter
- ½ cup white wine
- 1 Tbsp flour
- 1 cup half & half
- 2 Tbsp chopped fresh parsley

For the egg puff: Preheat oven to 350°F. Spray 4 individual ramekins with nonstick cooking spray. Combine all egg puff ingredients and mix well. Divide egg mixture among ramekins. Bake for about 30 minutes, or until golden brown.

For the white wine sauce: Combine butter and wine in saucepan over medium heat. Bring to a boil. Gradually add flour while whisking briskly. Remove pan from heat and add half & half, whisking until smooth. Fold in parsley. Serve warm. Drizzle each serving with white wine sauce and serve.

At Cumberland Falls Bed and Breakfast Inn

Crab Quiche Extraordinaire

Yield: 6 servings

1½ cups shredded sharp cheddar cheese (good quality required)
2 Tbsp flour
1½ cups half & half (or any kind of milk)
4 eggs, beaten well
1 (6-oz.) pkg. frozen crab or substitute
½ cup green onion, sliced
½ tsp salt
Dash white pepper
Dash Tabasco Sauce
1 pastry shell (homemade or store bought)

Preheat oven to 350°F. Toss the cheese with flour. Add half & half or desired milk, eggs, crab, onion, and seasonings and mix well. Pour into pastry shell and bake for 55–60 minutes or until set.

Tip: Old Bay, basil, oregano, cayenne, and lemon thyme are but a few of the many appropriate choice of seasonings one can use with eggs.

Hill House B&B
Egg and Asparagus Tart

Yield: 8 servings

 1 sheet puff pastry
 4 oz. chèvre cheese
 4 oz. cream cheese
 2 Tbsp chives, finely chopped
 1 clove garlic, minced
 8 spears asparagus, blanched and cut in ½-inch slices
 8 slices bacon, cooked and crumbled
16 eggs
    Salt and pepper to taste

Preheat oven to 375°F. Thaw puff pastry sheet according to package instructions. With a rolling pin and flour, roll pastry sheet to expand roughly ⅓ in size (enough to serve 8). Wet fingers with water and fold edges over ½ inch to form a crust. Bake on a lightly greased sheet pan for 12 minutes.

Mix cheeses, chives, and garlic in a small bowl until soft enough to spread.

The sheet will puff while baking; press the portion that's inside the crust down with a fork or spoon. Spread cheese mixture to cover pastry. Sprinkle with asparagus and bacon. Carefully crack eggs directly onto tart. Bake until whites have set but yolks are still runny (approximately 15–20 minutes). Allow to cool for a couple minutes, then cut into 8 slices and serve.

1906 Pine Crest Inn
Eggs Benedict

Yield: 3–4 servings

"This is 'our take' on eggs Benedict. We love to let the season dictate how this dish manifests in the use of local and seasonal flavors. Spring might provide a layer of crisp asparagus or tender baby spinach. Summer's bounty might prompt a fine slice of heirloom tomato or regional farmer's cheese. The autumn could provide savory butternut squash. And winter might encourage the use of earthy beets or even a roasted root vegetable hollandaise. Regardless, it's the quality of the biscuit that makes this dish a success."—Innkeeper

Biscuit:
- 2 cups White Lily flour
- ½ cup of vegetable shortening or lard
- 1 ½–2 cups buttermilk

- Free range eggs (6–8)
- water
- white vinegar

Hollandaise Sauce:
- 3 egg yolks
- ¼ tsp salt
- pinch of pepper—cayenne is great!
- 1–2 Tbsp of freshly squeezed lemon juice
- ½ cup unsalted butter

Filling:
Thinly sliced, NC country ham, Canadian bacon, NC smoked trout, Neese's country sausage, or your choice of seasonal fillings that has been warmed through.

(Continued next page)

Eggs Benedict *(Continued)*

Preheat oven to 450° F. Grease a baking sheet or line with parchment. In a large mixing bowl, cut the shortening into the sifted flour. You can use a pastry cutter but we like to do it by hand. The mixture should resemble coarse crumbs. Using one hand to mix, incorporate the buttermilk. Stir the milk into the flour, slowly bringing the flour in from the sides to create a moist dough. When the bulk of the flour has been incorporated into the dough (it will be a bit sticky), place it onto the work surface that has been dusted with flour. Bring the dough into a ball and knead for a few turns to create a smooth ball. On the well-floured surface, flatten the dough to a thickness of about ½ inch. Use a round cutter or pinch into balls for a more rustic look to make the biscuits. Place on baking sheet and place in hot oven. Bake for 12–15 minutes until golden brown. Brush with melted butter once out of the oven.

Bring a large saucepan of water to a boil and then reduce to a simmer. Add one tablespoon of white vinegar to the water. Break the eggs into a saucer and slide carefully into the simmering water. Do not allow to boil. Use a spoon to move water over the top of each yolk to help in setting the egg. Cook until the white of the egg is set, about 3 minutes. Remove from water with a slotted spoon and transfer to a bowl of ice water. Eggs can be held for an hour or more. When ready to serve, slide eggs back into hot water just long enough to warm through. Lift from water and drain on paper toweling before assembly.

For the hollandaise, place the egg yolks, salt, pepper, and lemon juice in a blender or food processor. Place the butter in a small saucepan and melt. Turn on the blender/processor and drizzle the melted butter by a thin stream in to the egg mixture. By the time ⅔ of the butter is incorporated into the sauce, it will be thick and creamy. Continue until all butter is used. Balance flavor with additional lemon juice, salt and pepper.

Assembly: Open two biscuits and place on serving plate. Top with filling of choice. Place a poached egg on top of each biscuit half. Spoon a dollop of hollandaise sauce over the egg. A sprinkle of paprika and a spring of fresh herb will make just the right presentation of this classic dish.

ROSEMARY HOUSE B&B
Eggs Benedict—Vegetarian Style

Yield: 4 servings

"All of these ingredients cook separately in five minutes or less."—Innkeeper

- 4 English muffins
- 8 eggs
- ½ lb. asparagus
- 1 (0.9 oz.) packet Knorr hollandaise sauce mix (uses butter and milk)
- 1 cup milk
- ¼ cup (½ stick) butter
  - tsp of dill or paprika (optional)

Start the water boiling to poach the eggs. In another pan, start water boiling to cook asparagus. In a third pan, whisk the milk into the hollandaise sauce mix and turn the burner on low. Crack eggs into poaching pan, cover, cook five minutes. Drop asparagus into boiling water for five minutes. Add butter to sauce and stir frequently as it melts; sauce will thicken. Toast English muffins. Assemble in this order: muffin, asparagus, egg, sauce. I sprinkle a pinch of dill or paprika on top.

Variation: substitute steamed spinach or fried mushrooms for the asparagus.

Morehead Manor B&B

Garden Vegetable Frittata

Yield: 6 servings

- 1 cup zucchini, shredded
- 1 cup cherry tomatoes, cut in half lengthwise
- ½ cup onion, chopped
- ⅓ cup grated Parmesan cheese
- 1 cup milk
- 2 eggs
- ½ cup baking mix (such as Bisquick)
- ½ tsp salt
- ¼ tsp pepper

Preheat oven to 400°F. Lightly grease six 6–8 ounce ramekins. Evenly sprinkle zucchini, tomato, onion, and cheese in the ramekins. In a medium bowl, stir together remaining ingredients until well blended. Evenly distribute over the vegetables and cheese in each of the ramekins. Bake uncovered 35–40 minutes or until tops are slightly golden. Cool 5 minutes. Garnish with tomato and parsley.

1906 Pine Crest Inn
Granny Smith Apple and Sweet Vidalia Onion Quiche

Yield: 6–8 servings

"This quiche has been a favorite of the 1906 Pine Crest Inn's guests for several years. Our Granny Smith apples come from nearby orchards in Flat Rock and Hendersonville, NC. The onions come from Vidalia, Georgia. This recipe took the Bronze Medal in the Select Registry "Inn-Credible Breakfast Cook-Off" National Culinary Competition in Williamsburg, VA, in 2008. We hope you enjoy it as much as we and our guests do!"—Innkeeper

2 cups flour	¼ tsp oregano (dried)
¼ tsp salt	2 large farm fresh eggs
¼ tsp dry mustard	½ cup heavy cream
½ lb. butter	1 tsp high quality Dijon mustard
3 tbsp cold water	¼ tsp sea salt
2 North Carolina Granny Smith apples	½ tsp freshly ground pepper
1 large Vidalia onion, julienne	½ cup shredded extra sharp cheddar cheese
3 tbsp unsalted butter	3 oz sliced extra sharp cheddar reserved for topping
2 tsp finely chopped fresh rosemary	Sprigs of fresh rosemary and basil for garnish
1½ tsp finely chopped fresh basil	
¼ tsp marjoram (dried)	

Preheat oven to 350°F. Stir together flour, salt, and dry mustard. Cut softened butter into the flour mixture, and add just enough water to form proper pastry consistency. Roll out dough and line 4 small tartlet pans. Allow these to stand while you prepare the apples and onions. After you have finished slicing apples and onions, place the crusts in the oven for about 8 minutes, or until lightly golden in color.

(Continued next page)

Granny Smith Apple and Sweet Vidalia Onion Quiche
(Continued)

Melt unsalted butter in sauté pan over medium heat. Add onion and cook, stirring with a wooden spoon until the onion begins to caramelize to a toffee brown. At this stage add the apples. They will begin to sweat. Allow to cook for a few minutes until the apple juice reduces and is absorbed by the onions. Remove from heat, add half of the herb mixture, and let stand.

In a bowl, whisk eggs until blended. Add heavy cream, remaining herb blend, Dijon mustard, salt, and pepper. When this is thoroughly blended add the shredded cheddar. Place apple and onion mix into prepared pie crusts to fill each dish 2/3 full and top with egg mixture. Cover the top of the quiche with sliced cheddar cheese and bake for approximately 15 minutes or until filling is set. Allow to stand for 5 minutes prior to serving.

Big Mill B&B
Grits & Sausage Breakfast Bake

Yield: 1 large 9-inch quiche or 2 smaller 7-inch quiches.

"I love to serve this recipe to my "Yankee" guests!"—Innkeeper

2	cups water
½	tsp salt
½	cup quick-cooking grits, not instant
1	lb. ground pork sausage
4	cups (8-oz.) yellow, shredded sharp cheddar cheese, divided
5–6	large eggs
1	cup milk
½	tsp dried thyme leaves

Preheat oven to 350°F or convection oven to 320°F. Grease one 9-inch deep dish or two 7-inch deep dish quiche dishes. Bring the water and salt to a boil. Add the grits and lower heat. Cook about 3 to 5 minutes, stirring occasionally until grits have thickened. Cool. *The grits must be cool so that they don't cook the eggs.* In a medium-size frying pan, cook sausage until done. Drain and crumble. Stir together the sausage and 3¾ cups shredded cheese. (Reserve ¼ cup of cheese for sprinkling on top.) In another bowl, whisk together the eggs and milk. Add the thyme. Add sausage-cheese mixture to the eggs. Stir in the cooled grits, breaking up any lumps. Pour into a greased 9-inch dish or two 7-inch dishes. Fill really full and then sprinkle the reserved ¼ cup cheese on top. Cook 45 minutes to 1 hour depending on your oven, or until a knife inserted into the center of the dish comes out clean. Sometimes it takes longer depending on how thick I make it. Dish will be golden brown and should not jiggle in the middle.

Tip: This dish is prettier when made with yellow cheese.

THE WHITE DOE INN
Maple Crunch Cereal

Yield: 6 to 7 Cups

"Served with just milk or topped with fresh fruit and yogurt, this cereal is packed full of all the right stuff for a busy day of sightseeing."—Innkeeper

2	cups old-fashioned rolled oats
4¼	cups wheat flakes cereal
1	Tbsp sesame seeds
⅓	cup sunflower seeds
⅓	cup shredded unsweetened coconut
1	cup chopped walnuts
⅓	cup maple syrup
⅓	cup sunflower oil

Preheat oven to 250°F. In a large bowl, combine oats, wheat flakes, sesame seeds, sunflower seeds, coconut, and walnuts. Heat maple syrup and sunflower oil in a small saucepan over low heat until thinned and combined; pour over oats mixture and mix well. Spread mixture on a large, rimmed baking sheet. Bake for 1 hour, turning frequently, until toasted all over. Cool and store in a large, airtight container.

Carol's Garden Inn
Maple Ham and Egg Cups

Yield: 6 servings

6   slices of deli ham
1   Tbsp maple syrup
6   eggs
1   Tbsp butter, melted
    Salt and pepper to taste

Preheat oven to 400°F. Brush inside of 6 muffin tins with melted butter. Line each tin with a piece of ham. Pour ½ teaspoon of maple syrup in each ham cup. Put one dab of butter in each ham cup. Crack one egg in each ham cup. Season with salt and pepper.

Bake for about 20 minutes, until eggs are set. Remove from oven. Twist ham cups gently to loosen from tins. Serve with biscuits.

Brookside Mountain Mist Inn B&B

Mexican Eggs Olé

Yield: 10 servings

"This is a great dish if you are making breakfast or brunch for a large group. We like to make it with diced ham for a more complete breakfast dish."—Innkeeper

16 oz. cottage cheese
1 cup milk
8 eggs
½ cup butter, melted
6–7 drops Tabasco Sauce
1 cup Bisquick
2 cups shredded cheddar cheese
11 oz. can Mexican corn, drained
salt
pepper
onion powder

Preheat oven to 350°F. Mix cottage cheese and milk together in a blender and set aside. Combine all other ingredients in a large bowl. Add cottage cheese mixture and stir well. Pour into a 9x11-inch greased baking dish. Bake for 50–55 minutes or until light golden brown. Serve with sour cream and salsa on the side.

Tip: You could also add bacon or ham (may need to cut back on salt).

1889 WhiteGate Inn & Cottage
Mushroom Tarragon Soufflé

Yield: 8 servings

16 extra large eggs, beaten
½ cup milk
½ tsp vanilla
½ tsp salt
½ tsp pepper
1 Tbsp Tarragon
2 cups grated Parmesan cheese
1½ cups sliced mushrooms (add mushrooms in morning)

Plan ahead—dish needs overnight refrigeration.

Preheat oven to 400°F. Generously spray 8 ramikins with nonstick cooking spray and dust with Parmesan cheese. Beat together first six ingredients. Add cheese and refrigerate overnight. Add mushrooms in the morning. Fill sprayed ramikins. Add ¼-inch hot water to bottom of a pan, place ramikins in the water, and bake for 40 minutes.

The Inn on Mill Creek
Orange Soufflé

Yield: 4–6 servings

"You will need a baking dish with steep sides for this recipe, or simply fill your baking dish ¾ full with batter to allow room for the soufflé to rise."—Innkeeper

Sauce

- 6 Tbsp butter
- ½ cup orange juice
- 2 Tbsp sugar

Batter

- 9 large eggs, separated into whites and yolks
- 7 Tbsp sugar
- ¼ cup orange juice
- 3 Tbsp all-purpose flour

Berry Topping

- 2 Tbsp butter
- 2 Tbsp sugar
- ½ cup orange juice
- 4 cups sliced strawberries

To make the sauce:

In a small or medium saucepan, melt butter. Add orange juice and sugar, removing from heat when bubbly.

Innkeeper Tip #1: You might want to make the sauce after you make the batter, because the sauce needs to be hot when it goes into the soufflé bowl. It goes in the dish first, before the batter, which is why we list it first.

To make the batter:

Separate yolks from the egg whites. In a large bowl, beat the egg whites until foamy. Add sugar and beat until the whites hold stiff peaks.

Innkeeper Tip #2: Do not overbeat the egg whites because that will make the mixture too thick … you need air in the mixture to help keep the soufflé's shape.

In a separate bowl, beat together the egg yolks, orange juice, and flour until well mixed. Gently fold into the egg whites with a rubber spatula (emphasis on gently).

Now, on to the soufflé! Preheat oven to 350°F. Spray your baking dish's sides with nonstick spray. Pour sauce into baking dish first. Gently slide large spoonfuls of the batter into the hot sauce. Bake for 45 minutes, or until the center jiggles only slightly.

To make topping (make 5–7 minutes before the soufflé comes out of the oven):

In a small or medium frying pan, melt butter. Stir in sugar and orange juice. When bubbling, stir in the sliced strawberries just until warm; do not cook. Spoon over soufflé before serving.

1906 Pine Crest Inn
Pine Crest Granola

Yield: 10–12 servings

4 cups rolled oats
2 cups chopped or sliced raw almonds
2 cups shredded coconut (natural or sweetened)
1 lb. salted butter, melted
1 Tbsp vanilla or almond flavoring
²/₃ cup brown sugar
1 Tbsp sea salt
2 cups dried tart cherries or golden raisins

Preheat oven to 350°F. In a large bowl, combine all ingredients except the cherries/raisins and mix thoroughly with hands. Spread onto a baking tray lined with parchment. Bake for 10 minutes then using a spatula turn the mixture on the pan. This promotes even browning. Continue baking and turning every 10 minutes until the mixture is golden brown. Remove from oven and stir in cherries/raisins. Cool on tray. Store in an airtight container.

Inn at Bingham School
Quiche Lorraine

Yield: 6 4½-inch individual quiches or 1 large quiche

"This recipe is simple if you use pre-made pastry. The real trick is to use the best eggs you can find, fresh from the farmers market is best. The same goes for the ham. I choose to make individual quiches because it is fun, but if you do not have the proper molds you may make 1 large quiche with the recipe."—Innkeeper

1	box Pillsbury pie crust or your favorite homemade one
¾	cup grated Swiss cheese
½	cup diced ham
3	large eggs, if using ungraded fresh market eggs use ¾ cup of eggs
1	cup heavy cream
½	tsp kosher salt
	Pinch white pepper
	Pinch nutmeg

Preheat oven to 375°F. Roll dough into tart pan with removable bottom, and follow package directions to blind bake. Place pre-baked shell(s) on baking sheet lined with parchment paper about 1 inch apart. Sprinkle cheese and ham evenly into shell(s). Whisk together in large mixing cup with spout, the eggs, cream, salt, pepper, and nutmeg. Slowly pour mixture into quiche shell(s) until it reaches top edge. Gently place sheet into oven. Bake 15 minutes, turn pan and bake until eggs are golden. I prefer to let quiche cool to room temperature before serving.

Tip: Do not relegate quiche to breakfast only—paired with salad and a glass of wine it makes a delicious lunch or light supper.

Lois Jane's Riverview Inn
Sausage & Egg Casserole
Yield: 10–12 servings

"Quick, easy, delicious, just right for any morning."—Innkeeper

  1 lb. bulk country sage sausage
  6 slices white bread, crusts removed
10 large eggs
  1 cup milk
  1 cup grated mild cheddar cheese
     Salt and black pepper, to taste

Preheat oven to 350°F. Crumble sausage into a skillet over medium heat and cook until browned. Place bread in a 9x13-inch baking dish. Sprinkle sausage over bread. Beat eggs, milk, cheese, salt and pepper; pour over sausage. Bake for about 30 minutes, until casserole is bubbling and cheese is melted.

Pamlico House B&B
Sun Dried Tomato & Cheddar Frittata

Yield: 12 servings

- 1 lb. extra sharp white cheddar cheese, grated (about 4 cups)
- ¾ cup chopped, drained, oil-packed sun-dried tomatoes
- ½ cup (packed) chopped fresh basil
- ½ cup chopped, drained, pickled jalapeño chilies from a jar (optional)
- 18 large eggs
- 5 Tbsp jalapeño liquid reserved (optional)

Preheat oven to 350°F. Spray nonstick spray on a 15x10x2-inch glass baking dish. Sprinkle cheese evenly over bottom. Sprinkle tomatoes and basil over cheese (jalapeños, too, if using). Using electric mixer, beat eggs in a large bowl until pale and slightly thickened, about 8 minutes. Beat in reserved 5 tablespoons jalapeño liquid (if using). Pour egg mixture evenly into dish. Bake until firm, about 30 minutes. Cool slightly and cut into 12 squares.

Tip: Can be made up to two days ahead, just cover and refrigerate. Can also be reheated at 350°F for 15–20 minutes, serve warm.

Inn on Main Street
Tofu Florentine

Yield: 2 servings

"This is an easy vegan adaptation if you are making eggs Florentine for other guests. The faux hollandaise sauce is so good that you can use it on eggs Florentine as well. Get nutritional yeast at any health food store."—Innkeeper

4 oz. extra firm tofu
1 tsp olive oil
¼ tsp Emeril's seasoning or another Cajun-style spice
¼ tsp salt
1 tsp whole-wheat flour
½ cup soy milk or almond milk
¼ cup nutritional yeast

¼ tsp salt
¼ tsp ground black pepper
¼ tsp dry tarragon
1 tsp lemon juice
1 oz. spinach, cooked and drained
2 English muffins, commercial or homemade

Preheat oven to 450°F. Cut tofu into four equal slices. In ovenproof dish, coat tofu slices on each side with olive oil, spread in pan and top with seasoning and salt. Bake for 10–15 minutes, turning once. Leave in warm oven until needed.

Meanwhile, in a small saucepan add flour and soy/almond milk. Mix well. Set over medium-high burner. Mix in yeast, salt, pepper, tarragon, and lemon juice. Bring to a boil, then immediately turn burner to low. Sauce should thicken some. Add more soy/almond milk if it gets too thick to pour. Warm cooked spinach in separate pan on stove or in oven.

Tear English muffins in half and toast. Top two halves on each plate with slices of tofu, then spinach, then a drizzle of faux hollandaise sauce. Serve immediately.

A BED OF ROSES, VICTORIAN B&B
Vegan Polenta Nests

Yield: 2 servings

Polenta

2 Tbsp soy or non-dairy butter
¼ cup minced scallions
1½ cups water
½ tsp salt
½ cup yellow cornmeal
¼ cup non-dairy Parmesan
1 tsp fresh thyme, minced

Filling

½ cup diced onion
¼ cup diced red peppers
¼ cup diced green peppers
½ cup Veggie Shreds, divided
2 sliced Smart Links or other brand non-meat breakfast sausage
1 tsp fresh thyme
black pepper

One or two days before serving, make the polenta. Melt non-dairy butter in a medium saucepan. Add scallions and sauté just until limp. Add the water and salt and bring to a boil. Gradually whisk in the corn meal and bring to a boil. Reduce heat to low and simmer until thick and creamy, about 10 minutes, stirring frequently. Stir in non-dairy Parmesan and fresh thyme. Season with salt and fresh ground pepper. Cool to room temperature, then cover and refrigerate at least overnight or for up to 2 days.

To Assemble the Nests:

Preheat oven to 400°F. Spray two 1-cup ramekins with nonstick cooking spray. Put about ⅓ cup of polenta into each ramekin, pressing into the bottom and up the sides to form a nest. Sprinkle ¼-cup of Veggie Shreds in each ramekin. Slice sausage substitute and sauté. Remove to a bowl. Sauté onion and peppers and add to sausage. Divide mixture between the polenta-lined ramekins. Sprinkle with remaining Veggie Shreds, scallions, thyme and black pepper. Place ramekins on a rimmed baking sheet and bake about 20–25 minutes.

803 Elizabeth B&B
Will's Granola

Yield: 16–20 servings

5 cups old-fashioned oatmeal
¾ cup shelled, raw, unsalted sunflower seeds
2 Tbsp cinnamon
1 cup total—⅓ each of honey, ⅓ cup agave and ⅓ cup maple syrup
⅓ cup canola oil
1 cup raw sliced almonds
1 cup pecans or walnuts, coarsely chopped
1 cup dates
1 cup craisins

Preheat oven to 325°F. Mix oats, sunflower seeds, cinnamon, and liquids. Let stand for at least 30 minutes. Spread in a 12x17-inch low-rimmed pan (jellyroll pan). Bake for approximately 25 minutes, stirring every 10 minutes. Add almonds and other nuts, and bake for an additional 5 minutes—do not overbrown.

Place pan on cooling rack and add dates, craisins, or other dried fruit. Mix carefully and allow to cool completely. Store in a tightly covered container. Can also be frozen.

Appetizers, Soups, Salads & Sides

THE MOSS HOUSE B&B
Beer Cheese Dip

Yield: approximately 2 cups

"This is a great recipe to double and share with friends! A real hit for a party and one of my families' favorite spreads!"—Innkeeper

- 8 oz. pkg. cream cheese (low-fat works fine), softened
- 8 oz. sharp cheddar, grated
- ¼ cup beer
- 1 clove garlic, minced or pressed
- 2 Tbsp Worchestershire sauce
- ½ tsp mustard
- ¼ tsp ground red pepper or to taste

Beat the cream and cheddar cheese with hand mixer until smooth. Gradually add some beer and all other ingredients. Chill overnight (or at least 2 hours) for flavors to blend. Remove from the refrigerator a half hour before serving. Serve with Fritos Scoops or your favorite crackers.

Tip: For a creamier texture, add more beer.

The Inn at Celebrity Dairy

Black Bean, Goat Cheese & Tomatillo Three-Layer Dip

Yield: 12 servings

1 lb. tomatillos
2 cloves garlic, minced
3 medium jalapeño peppers, halved and seeded
1 tsp salt
   Juice of ½ lemon
2 cups dehydrated black bean mix
2 cups boiling water
8 oz. goat cheese, crumbled
   Cilantro leaves, for garnish
   Tortilla chips, for serving

Remove papery husks from tomatillos then wash, dry, and quarter them. Place them and the garlic, jalapeños, salt and lemon juice in a food processor; purée, then chill for at least 30 minutes (or overnight). Put black bean mix on a large platter (about 12-inches in diameter). Pour boiling water over black bean mix and stir with a fork until combined. Strain excess liquid from tomatillo mixture and spread over black beans. Top with crumbled goat cheese. Sprinkle with cilantro and serve with tortilla chips.

Morning Glory Inn
Hot Crab Dip

Yield: approximately 4 cups

2	(8-oz.) pkgs. cream cheese
1–2	Tbsp grated onion
1	tsp creamy style horeseradish
	dash of Tabasco Sauce
	salt and pepper to taste
12–15	oz. can crabmeat
	dash of paprika

Preheat oven to 350°F. Heat cream cheese in large mixing bowl in microwave for 35 seconds, then 25 seconds more. Stir until smooth. Add rest of ingredients, except crab and paprika, and mix well. Add crabmeat and stir thoroughly. Spread in small casserole/serving dish and sprinkle with paprika. Bake for 20 to 30 minutes or until bubbling on edges. Serve warm with crackers or pita chips.

Arrowhead Inn
Smoky Black Bean Dip

Yield: 3 cups

4	slices bacon
1	medium onion, chopped
1	red bell pepper, chopped
½	tsp ground cumin
½	tsp dried oregano
2	(15-oz.) cans black beans, drained
1	Tbsp chopped chipotle peppers (canned)
	Salt and black pepper, to taste
½	cup sour cream
2	tsp chopped fresh cilantro
	Tortilla chips, for serving

Cook bacon in a large skillet over medium heat until crisp; coarsely chop bacon and set aside. Pour off all but 1 tablespoon of bacon drippings from skillet. Add onion and bell pepper to skillet and cook for about 6 minutes, until onion is soft. Add cumin and oregano; cook for 1 minute. Add black beans and chipotle peppers. Lower heat to medium-low and simmer for about 4 minutes, stirring occasionally, until slightly thickened.

Transfer black bean mixture to a food processor or blender and process until smooth. Season with salt and pepper. Put black bean mixture in a bowl, cover and refrigerate for 2 hours. (The dip can be made up to 2 days ahead—cover and chill dip and bacon separately.)

Add half of the bacon to dip and stir to combine. Top with sour cream. Sprinkle with cilantro and remaining bacon. Serve chilled or at room temperature with tortilla chips.

BIG MILL B&B

Cheese Crackers

Yield: 2 cookie sheets or about 100 cookies

"Perfect for nibbling."—Innkeeper

- 2 cups sharp cheddar cheese, shredded
- 2 sticks margarine (NOT spread)
- 2 cups all-purpose flour
- ½ tsp cayenne pepper
- 2 cups Rice Krispies
  Beau Monde seasoning

Preheat oven to 350°F. Cream the cheese and margarine together with a fork or in a mixer. Mix flour and cayenne together in another bowl. Add to cheese mixture. Stir in Rice Krispies 1 cup at a time. (If you want to make ahead, mix all but the Rice Krispies, add just before baking).

Roll mixture into marble-sized balls and put on ungreased cookie sheet. Flatten with a fork into flat penny-shaped cracker. Sprinkle with Beau Monde seasoning.

Bake approximately 12 minutes until light brown. Remove from oven before they are completely brown. Pennies will continue to cook after they are removed from oven. They are crispy when done. Cool and store in air-tight container.

Tips: This is one time that orange cheese is better to use. Land O' Lakes makes a stick margarine. Use ¼ tsp cayenne if you don't like the "bite." Beau Monde seasoning is available in the spice section of the grocery store. To make your own, mix ½ cup celery salt, and ¼ cup onion powder.

Big Mill B&B
Pimento Cheese

Yield: 6–10 servings

"Pimento Cheese, our Southern patê, is comfort food for those of us who live south of the Mason Dixon line. It usually shows up in a blue Tupperware dish with the name Beulah, Pearl, or Lurlene written on the bottom … or whichever aunt made it. It is customarily spread on white bread, stuffed into celery stalks, or on toast. It always shows up at "Dinner on the Grounds" and at funerals. In Being Dead is no Excuse, the Official Southern Ladies Guide to Hosting a Perfect Funeral, *there are six different pimento cheese recipes. Sometimes we even cut the crusts off the bread and then cut the sandwich into four triangles—we do this at weddings and when we are trying to impress our city cousins or new in-laws."*—Innkeeper

1½	cups sharp, white cheddar cheese, coarsely grated
1½	cups sharp, yellow cheddar cheese, coarsely grated
1	(4-oz.) jar diced or chopped pimentos
3	dashes of sea salt
¼	tsp ground cayenne pepper
½	cup Duke's mayonnaise

Drain the pimentos and squeeze out any excess liquid. Gently stir together the cheeses (I use only Cabot's), pimentos, salt, and cayenne pepper. Add the mayonnaise. In the South, folks swear by Dukes mayonnaise so that is what I use. Do not over-stir because the pimento cheese will become mushy. You may have to add a wee bit more mayonnaise on the second day.

To serve: At Big Mill we serve Chloe's homemade pimento cheese with pita points, toasted crisp in the oven.

Tip: Go light on the cayenne if you don't like food with a "bite."

1906 Pine Crest Inn
Pine Crest Pimento Cheese

Yield: 6–10 servings (depending on portion size for appetizer or sandwich)

- 8 oz. cream cheese, at room temperature
- 10 oz. white Vermont Cheddar, grated
- ¼ medium onion, grated
- 1 (2-oz.) jar chopped pimentos
- ½ cup Duke's mayonnaise
- 2 Tbsp sweet pickle juice
- 1 Tbsp Texas Pete® or other red pepper sauce
- salt and pepper to taste

In a medium bowl combine the softened cream cheese with the grated cheddar. Place the grated onion into the corner of a clean kitchen cloth and squeeze the juice of the onion into the bowl. Stir in remaining ingredients to achieve a smooth consistency. Season to taste. If the mixture is too stiff and not creamy, add additional mayonnaise to achieve a creamy consistency.

Serve with fresh crudités, crisp baguette slices, or artisan crackers. This delicious Southern spread may also be used for sensational grilled cheese sandwiches or atop fried green tomatoes.

803 Elizabeth B&B
Spinach Brownies

Yield: About 20 squares

"Makes a great appetizer—something different that can be served hot or cold."—Innkeeper

¼	cup butter
½	cup chopped onion
1	pkg. frozen spinach, thawed
1	cup whole wheat flour
1	tsp baking soda
½	tsp nutmeg
2	eggs
1	cup milk
2–3	cups grated cheese (about ¾ lb.)

Preheat oven to 350°F. Melt butter in frying pan and cook onions in butter until translucent. Add thawed spinach and heat until liquid is gone.

In a bowl, mix together flour, soda, and nutmeg. In a separate bowl, mix the eggs, milk and add to flour mixture. Add onion and spinach from frying pan. Add cheese, mix well, and place in a greased 8x11 or 9x13-inch dish or pan. Bake for 35 minutes or until lightly browned.

Allow to cool slightly and cut in squares. Can be frozen after cooking and reheated at 350°F for 10 minutes.

Andon-Reid Inn B&B
Spinach, Crab & Artichoke Mini Tarts

Yield: 12 servings

"These are wonderful appetizers. I serve these with our 'Wine Down.'"—Innkeeper

3 Tbsp mayonnaise
3 Tbsp sour cream
Generous dash freshly ground black pepper
¼ cup frozen chopped spinach, thawed and well-drained
⅓ cup well-drained, chopped, canned artichoke heart
⅓ cup lump crabmeat, well-drained

½ of a 17.3-oz. pkg. Pepperidge Farm® Puff Pastry Sheets (1 sheet), thawed
3 Tbsp Japanese bread crumbs (Panko)
1½ Tbsp Parmigiano-Reggiano or Parmesan cheese, finely grated
1½ tsp extra-virgin olive oil
12 small sprigs fresh parsley

Preheat oven to 375°F. In a medium bowl, mix the mayonnaise, sour cream, and black pepper. Add the spinach, artichokes, crabmeat, and mix lightly.

Unfold the pastry sheet on a lightly floured surface. Cut the pastry sheet into three 2½-inch wide strips. Discard the remaining pastry. Cut each pastry strip into four 2½-inch squares, making 12 in all. Press the pastry squares into 12 (1¾-inch) mini-muffin pan cups. Spoon 1½ tablespoons crab mixture into each pastry cup. In a small bowl, mix the bread crumbs, cheese and oil. Sprinkle 1 teaspoon bread crumb mixture over each filled pastry. Bake for 20 minutes or until the pastries are golden brown. Top each with 1 sprig of parsley before serving.

THE INN AT CELEBRITY DAIRY

Butternut Squash Soup

Yield: 10 servings

"We serve this soup topped with fresh goat yogurt or goat curd thinned to the consistency of heavy cream."—Innkeeper

1 large butternut squash
2 Tbsp vegetable oil
2 medium onions, chopped
2 cloves garlic, minced
1 large red bell pepper, minced
½ tsp cumin
½ tsp coriander
½ tsp ground ginger
½ tsp dry mustard
½ tsp curry powder

1½ tsps salt
1 cup orange juice
Juice and grated zest of 1 lemon
¼ tsp cayenne pepper or hot sauce
1 (14½-oz.) can corn, drained
Fresh goat yogurt or curd (thinned to consistency of heavy cream), for serving

Preheat oven to 425°F. Cut squash in half lengthwise and scoop out seeds. Put squash in a baking dish with 1-inch of water. Bake for about 1 hour, until tender. Peel and cube squash, then purée in a food processor or blender in batches (using 1 cup of squash and up to 1 cup of squash cooking liquid or water to thin per batch).

Heat oil in a skillet over medium heat. Add onions, garlic and bell pepper; cook until onions are translucent. Transfer squash and onion mixture to a soup pot. Add cumin, coriander, ginger, mustard, curry powder and salt. Bring to a boil, lower heat and simmer for 20 minutes. Add orange and lemon juices, lemon zest, cayenne and corn. Simmer for 10 minutes. Serve topped with goat yogurt or curd (be careful, this soup retains a lot of heat, so don't serve it too hot).

Home Coming Bed and Breakfast

Can Can Soup

Yield: 6 servings

"An easy dish that can be prepared in a hurry."—Innkeeper

2 cans Campbell's tomato soup
   Splash of Texas Pete®
1 can Veg-All chunky mixed vegetables
¼ lb. ground beef, browned and drained
   tomato juice for desired consistency

Empty tomato soup in a pot and add a splash of Texas Pete. Add tomato juice to desired consistency. Add browned ground beef and Veg-All. Stir extremely well, bring to a hard boil and turn heat down to simmer until you're ready to serve.

Note: For the story on Texas Pete, see page 287.

OLD NORTH DURHAM INN
Curried Parsnip Soup

Yield: 6 servings

4 cups chicken stock
2 oz. (½ stick) butter
1 cup (scant) chopped onion
1 clove garlic, minced
13 oz. parsnip, peeled and chopped
1 Tbsp plus 1 tsp flour
1 tsp curry powder
2 cups half & half
chopped chives or parsley as garnish

In a saucepan, heat the chicken stock. In a heavy-bottomed saucepan melt the butter. Add the onion, garlic, and parsnip. Season with salt and freshly ground pepper. Toss until well coated. Cover and cook on a gentle heat until soft and tender, about 10 minutes. Stir in flour and curry powder. Gradually incorporate hot chicken stock. Simmer until the parsnips are fully cooked. Liquidize, taste and correct the seasoning. Add half & half to taste. Sprinkle with finely chopped chives or parsley. Serve with crispy croutons.

The Lamplight Inn
Chicken & Wild Rice Salad

Yield: 6–8 servings

"A lovely blend of favors. Canned tuna may be substituted for the chicken. Plan ahead as this salad needs to marinate overnight."—Innkeeper

1 pkg. Good Seasons Italian dressing mix
2 (10-oz.) pkgs. Uncle Ben's wild rice mix
1 cup mayonnaise
5 boneless, skinless chicken breasts, cooked and cut up
1 (4-oz.) jar pimentos
1 (6-oz.) jar water-packed artichoke hearts, drained
2 cups finely chopped celery
2 cups finely chopped green bell pepper
1 (10½-oz.) pkg. frozen peas (optional)
1 lb. fresh mushrooms, sliced

Prepare salad dressing and cook rice according to package directions. Mix salad dressing, rice, mayonnaise and chicken; cover and refrigerate overnight.

The next day, stir pimentos, artichokes, celery, bell pepper, and peas into rice mixture. Stir in mushrooms not more than 30 minutes before serving.

803 Elizabeth B&B
Cucumber Salad

Yield: 6–8 servings

2 medium cucumbers
1 large sweet onion
   kosher salt
2 Tbsp dill

Dressing
2 Tbsp vinegar
2 heaping Tbsp plain yogurt

Thinly slice cucumbers and onion, and alternate layers in a bowl. Sprinkle kosher salt (or whatever salt you prefer) on each layer. Weigh down with heavy dish—I use a plate that rests on the cucumbers and put something heavy on it for additional weight. Refrigerate for several hours or overnight. Drain once or twice. You will be surprised at the amount of water!

In a colander wash the cucumbers thoroughly with running water. Taste to make sure they are not too salty! Drain well and place cucumbers and onions in a bowl. A couple of hours before serving, mix with vinegar yogurt dressing. (You can add more vinegar or yogurt according to your taste.) Just before serving sprinkle 2 tablespoons of coarsely chopped dill on top.

THE LAMPLIGHT INN
Cranberry Chutney

Yield: 5–6 cups

"Cranberries never tasted so good—this recipe always gets rave reviews."—Innkeeper

1 cup chopped peeled orange
¼ cup orange juice
4 cups fresh or frozen cranberries
2 cups sugar
½ cup raisins
1 cup chopped unpeeled apple
½ tsp cinnamon
½ tsp ground ginger
1 Tbsp apple cider vinegar
½ cup chopped nuts

Combine all ingredients in a large saucepan over medium-high heat. Bring to a boil, then lower heat and simmer for 10 minutes, or until cranberries burst. Chill until serving.

1906 Pine Crest Inn
Fruited Tuna Salad

Yield: 2 servings (as a lunch entrée or four as sandwiches)

6 oz. albacore tuna packed in water
½ cup finely chopped dried apricots
½ cup finely chopped red onion
½ cup Duke's mayonnaise
½ tsp Chinese Five-spice powder
   salt and pepper to taste
   poppy seeds

Drain tuna and flake into mixing bowl. Combine all ingredients and season with salt and pepper. Serve with crisp Bibb lettuce or perhaps some spicy arugula that has been lightly dressed with fresh lemon juice and olive oil accompanied by fresh melon and radishes. Top with poppy seeds.

OLD NORTH DURHAM INN
Mom's Squash Fritters

Yield: about 12

*"Great recipe for all that squash that seems
to pile up during the summer."*—Innkeeper

1 egg
⅓ cup milk
1 Tbsp vegetable oil
1 cup flour
½ tsp salt
1 Tbsp sugar
1 tsp baking powder
2 yellow squash, medium-sized
Vegetable shortening

Mix first three ingredients in a small bowl. Mix dry ingredients in a
separate large bowl. Just before cooking, grate squash (including skin)
and add to dry ingredients, along with the liquid mixture. Drop by
heaping tablespoons into a preheated (375°F) skillet, filled with ¼-inch
of vegetable shortening. Fry until light brown and puffy, then turn to
brown second side.

Lodge on Lake Lure
North Carolina Apple Chutney

Yield: 4 cups

1	medium red onion, diced
	Zest and juice of 1 orange, divided
1	tsp dried thyme
1	bay leaf
4	North Carolina Gala apples, peeled, cored and diced
1	tsp cinnamon
¼	cup dried cranberries
¼	cup currants
¼	cup golden raisins
¼	cup plus 2 Tbsp champagne vinegar
½	cup clover honey
¼	cup fresh lemon juice
1	cup chopped walnuts, toasted

Combine onion, orange zest, thyme, and bay leaf in a skillet over medium heat; cook, stirring frequently, for 8–10 minutes, until onions are soft. Stir in apples, cinnamon, dried cranberries, currants, and raisins; cook for 3 minutes. Stir in vinegar, honey, and orange and lemon juices; cook for 5 minutes. Stir in walnuts. Serve warm over pork or chicken.

Note: This chutney may be made several days in advance, covered and refrigerated. Reheat the chutney when ready to serve.

Pamlico House B&B
Port Lime Syrup

Yield: approximately ½ cup

"Great with any fruit, I usually serve it with cantaloupe and/or honeydew melons garnished with a strawberry."—Innkeeper

2 Tbsp water
¼ cup sugar
3 Tbsp fresh lime juice
2 Tbsp tawny port
   zest of 1 lime

Mix sugar and water in a saucepan and stir until dissolved while simmering on low heat for 2 minutes. Remove from heat and add remaining ingredients, except zest. Can be made in advance up to this point.

For serving, pour syrup over fruit, sprinkle with zest, and serve.

A tawny port, tawny in color and ready to drink when bottled, is made from a blend of grapes from several different years and can be aged in wood for as long as 40 years.

Beaufort House Inn
Pumpkin Spice Yogurt

Yield: 4–6 (1 cup) servings

*"Wonderful and easy for breakfast and/or brunch
in the fall and winter months."*—Innkeeper

　　toasted chopped pecans
1　cup canned pumpkin pie mix (spices already included)
3　cups Brown Cow brand Cream on Top vanilla yogurt
　　good quality organic granola

Lightly toast chopped pecans in a 350°F oven for about 15 minutes.
Set aside to cool. In a large bowl whisk together the pumpkin pie mix
and the yogurt until very well blended. This can be prepared the night
before and placed in a sealed container.

Serve pumpkin spice yogurt in martini glasses for a fun presentation or
individual serving dish of your choice. Top with toasted pecans.

ROSEMARY HOUSE B&B
Roasted Portabello Napoleon

Yield: 6 servings

6 Portabello mushrooms
¼ cup olive oil
¼ cup balsamic vinegar
1 tsp pepper
1 tsp salt
2 cloves garlic
½ tsp marjoram
1 Tbsp Italian herbs
1 cup quinoa

4 cups fresh spinach
1½ cups good quality
   balsamic vinegar (not the
   most expensive but not
   the cider vinegar-corn
   syrup-food coloring kind)
2 Tbsp sugar
½ jar roasted red peppers

Remove stems from mushrooms (save for another use). Combine olive oil, vinegar, salt, pepper, garlic, marjoram, Italian herbs, and mushrooms in a bowl. Let the mushrooms marinate in the dressing for 2 hours. To roast mushrooms, preheat oven to 425 degrees. Cover a baking sheet with tinfoil sprayed with nonstick spray. Arrange Portabello mushrooms on the foil. Place the pan in the oven and roast for 20 minutes. Cook quinoa according to package directions. (Exactly like rice, 2 cups water to one cup quinoa, simmer very low for 20 minutes.) To sauté spinach, heat 2 Tbsp olive oil over medium heat (not sizzling). Add the spinach and cook for about two minutes. To reduce the vinegar, boil it with the sugar until it is reduced to ½ cup. (Mark the level before-hand on a chopstick, using a measured half-cup of water.)

For each Napoleon, assemble in this order, bottom to top:

½ cup cooked quinoa
1 roasted mushroom
1/3 cup sautéed spinach
3 slivers of roasted red pepper
1½ Tbsp balsamic vinegar reduction (drizzled over)

THE TROTT HOUSE INN
Sausage in Puff Pastry

Yield: 12 servings

1 lb. bulk pork sausage
1 medium onion, chopped
½ cup grated cheddar cheese
1 medium apple, peeled and grated
2 Tbsp chopped fresh sage or 2 tsp dried sage
1 (17-oz.) pkg. frozen puff pastry, thawed
2 Tbsp milk

Preheat oven to 400°F. Brown sausage and onion in a skillet over medium heat, breaking up sausage as it cooks; drain well. Combine sausage mixture, cheese, apple, and sage; mix well and set aside.

On a lightly floured surface, roll out 1 sheet of puff pastry into a 10x15-inch rectangle. Spread half of sausage mixture lengthwise down center of puff pastry. Cut puff pastry from the edges to the filling into 1-inch-wide strips. Fold alternating strips of puff pastry over filling in a criss-cross pattern. Brush ends with milk and seal. Repeat with remaining pastry and sausage mixture (if remaining pastry is too soft to handle, refrigerate for 5–10 minutes first).

Using 2 large spatulas, carefully transfer pastries to a greased baking pan or baking sheet. Brush pastries with remaining milk. Bake for 25–30 minutes, or until golden brown. Refrigerate leftovers.

Tip: Unbaked pastry rolls can be wrapped and frozen for up to 1 week. Bake frozen pastry rolls for 30–38 minutes, or until golden brown.

Lunch & Dinner Entrées

Buffalo Tavern B&B
ABC Casserole Bake

Yield: 8 generous servings

3–4	Granny Smith apples, sliced as desired
2	cups shredded cheddar cheese
2	pkgs. (2.5-oz. each) real bacon bits
16	eggs
4	Tbsp sour cream
½	cup Bisquick

Preheat oven to 375°F. Spray a 13x9-inch baking dish with nonstick spray. Line bottom of dish with generous amount of apples. Spread cheddar cheese on top of apples. Spread the bacon bits on top of the cheese. In a bowl, mix the eggs, sour cream, and Bisquick. Pour over ABC (apples, bacon, cheese) ingredients.

Bake for 45 minutes or until a toothpick comes out clean.

ROSEMARY HOUSE B&B
Asparagus Enchiladas

Yield: 6 generous servings

12 flour tortillas (8-inch)	1 jar (8-oz.) salsa
2 lbs. asparagus	2 cups shredded
¼ cup butter	Swiss cheese
¼ cup flour	1 large onion
3 cups vegetable broth	1 cup chopped parsley
1 cup sour cream	

Preheat oven to 250°F. Wrap the tortillas in a damp dishtowel, cover in foil, and warm in the oven for 20 minutes before filling. Trim the asparagus ends. In a large pot filled with lightly salted boiling water, cook asparagus until barely tender, about 3 minutes. Drain, rinse under cold water, and drain again. In a large saucepan, melt butter over medium heat. Add flour and cook, stirring, for 1–2 minutes; add the broth all at once and bring to a boil, whisking, for about 3 or 4 minutes or until sauce is thick and smooth. Remove from heat. Stir in the sour cream, salsa, and Swiss cheese.

Remove the warm tortillas from the oven. Increase oven heat to 400°F (unless freezing the dish for later cooking.) Cover the bottom of a 13x9-inch baking dish with a thin layer of the sauce. Distribute the asparagus to the tortillas. Add to each one a little chopped onion, a little chopped parsley, and a tablespoon of the cheese sauce. Roll up carefully and set snugly in the baking dish, seam-side down. Continue filling and rolling tortillas until all tortillas and filling ingredients are used up. Pour remaining cheese sauce over all. Cover the baking dish with aluminum foil. (At this point you can refrigerate or freeze this dish if you wish.) Bake for 20–25 minutes, or until hot and bubbly.

THE SUNSET INN
Baked Cheese Grits Casserole

Yield: 8–10 servings

1½ cups grits
 1 lb. sausage or 12 sausage patties, crumbled
12 eggs, beaten
 1 can evaporated milk
 1 box Jiffy corn muffin mix
 8 oz. cream cheese
 8 cups shredded cheese, divided
   Salt and pepper to taste

Preheat oven to 350°F. In a saucepan, cook the grits in 6 cups of water. Brown sausage or use Jimmy Dean precooked sausage and crumble. In a large bowl, add milk to beaten eggs and blend in the corn muffin mix with a whisk and set aside. Add the cream cheese, 4 cups of cheese, and sausage to the cooked grits. Blend well and stir into the milk/eggs/corn muffin mix. Blend well and pour into a 11x15-inch baking dish that has been sprayed with baking or cooking spray. Top with remaining four cups of cheese and bake for one hour. It will puff up and a knife inserted should come out clean when done. Feel free to put foil over after about 45 minutes to keep the cheese from burning.

For a 9x13 pan, change ingredients to:

    1 cup grits and 4 cups water
    6 eggs
    1 cup evaporated milk
    6 oz. corn muffin mix
    4 to five cups shredded cheese (divided)
4 to 5 oz. cream cheese

ROSEMARY HOUSE
Black Bean-Sweet Potato Chili

Yield: 6 servings

2 Tbsp olive oil
2 medium onions, finely chopped
¼ cup water
3 cloves garlic, minced
1 red bell pepper, chopped
1 (64-oz.) can low-sodium tomato juice
2 Tbsp chili powder
2 tsp cumin
½ teaspoon cayenne red pepper
2 (15-oz.) cans peeled and diced tomatoes
3 large sweet potatoes, peeled, diced into ½-inch pieces
2 (15-oz.) cans black beans, drained, rinsed
¼ cup chopped cilantro

In a large pot, heat the oil over medium-low heat, add the onions and ¼ cup water. Cover pan and cook 5 minutes, stirring occasionally. Add the garlic and bell pepper with about ½ cup of the tomato juice. Cover and cook 5 minutes, stirring occasionally. Stir in the chili powder, cumin, and cayenne; stir 1 minute. Then add the remaining tomato juice, tomatoes, and sweet potatoes. Bring to a boil, cover and reduce the heat to a simmer. Cook 20 minutes, stirring occasionally. Stir in the black beans and simmer, uncovered, 15 minutes. Stir in the cilantro and serve with corn chips or over rice.

FUQUAY MINERAL SPRING INN

Cedar Plank Grilled Salmon with a Roasted Yellow Pepper-Saffron Sauce

Yield: 8 servings

For the Sauce

3 Tbsp olive oil
1 large yellow onion, coarsely chopped
3 yellow bell peppers, roasted, peeled, and coarsely chopped
1 cup dry white wine
large pinch of saffron threads
¾ cup heavy cream
salt and pepper to taste

Heat the olive oil in a medium saucepan over medium-high heat. Add onion and cook until soft. Add roasted peppers and cook for 10 minutes. In a small bowl, combine the wine and saffron. Add the wine mixture to the onion mixture and raise the heat, cook until almost dry. Pour mixture into a blender and blend until smooth. Place mixture into a clean saucepan over medium heat, add cream and simmer about 10 minutes. Season to taste with salt and pepper. Makes about 3 cups.

For the Salmon

About 10 untreated cedar shims (at most lumberyards)
Vegetable oil for cedar
8 salmon fillets, 6 oz. each
olive oil for salmon
salt and pepper to taste

Preheat a gas grill to medium heat, or prepare a charcoal fire. Soak the cedar shims in water for 1 hour. Remove shims and brush with vegetable oil on both sides. Place shims on the grill and allow to heat up about 5 minutes. Brush each side of the salmon with olive oil and season with salt and pepper to taste. Place salmon on the cedar and grill until medium-well done, about 8 to 10 minutes. Remove salmon from the shims and place on serving platter. Spoon with the warm sauce.

CAROL'S GARDEN INN
Creamy Shrimp and Rice

Yield: 4 servings

 2 tsp olive oil
½ cup chopped red peppers
½ cup chopped onion
 1 (6-oz.) pkg. sugar snap peas, halved
 1 lb. frozen cooked, cleaned medium shrimp, thawed, drained
¼ tsp black pepper
¼ cup milk
 1 (10-oz.) tub Philadelphia Savory Garlic Cooking Cream
 2 cups hot cooked long-grain white rice

Heat oil in large skillet on medium high heat. Add red peppers and onions and cook, stirring 4 to 5 minutes or until crisp tender. Stir in peas, cook 3 to 4 minutes or until heated through, stirring frequently. Add shrimp, black pepper, and milk, cook and stir 3 minutes or until heated through. Add cooking cream. Serve over rice.

Beaufort House Inn

Fresh Vegetable Crêpes served with Parmesan Béchamel Sauce & Parmesan Crisp Cookie

Yield: 8–10 servings (two crêpes per serving)

Parmesan Crisp Cookies:

2	cups shredded Parmesan cheese
6	zucchini
6	summer squash
6	sweet red peppers
24	asparagus spears (3 per serving)

Parmesan Béchamel Sauce:

1	stick butter
1	cup all-purpose flour
4	cups half & half cream
2	Tbsp ground nutmeg
1	cup grated Parmesan cheese

Crêpe Batter:

5	eggs
2	cups cold water
2½	cups half & half
4	cups malted flour (Carbon Brand)
2	sticks melted butter

(Continued next page)

Crêpes *(Continued)*

Parmesan Cookie Crisp: Place 4 Tbsp shredded Parmesan on a hot griddle and flatten into small, flat round. When golden brown on underside, flip to other side. Remove when both sides are golden and place on paper towel until serving time. Repeat to create one per serving.

Fresh Vegetables: Preheat oven to 400°F. Large chop all vegetables, but asparagus stay whole. Roast with olive oil and salt in oven until lightly golden, about 20–30 minutes. Keep warm.

Béchamel Sauce: Melt 1 stick of butter in saucepan—when golden brown, add 1 cup all-purpose flour. Whisk to make a classic roux. Let simmer for 5 minutes. Add half & half cream and whisk on low heat until desired thickness and smoothness. Add nutmeg and grated Parmesan and whisk until blended. If too thick before serving, adjust with more cream.

Crêpe Batter: Whisk eggs until frothy. Add water and half & half and whisk to combine. Add malted flour and melted butter and whisk gently to combine. With a 1/3 cup dry measure, ladle crêpe batter onto hot griddle (400°). When bubbles form on top, flip and cook on other side. Stack crêpes in a deep lidded pot on stovetop—this keeps them hot and soft.

Presentation:

Place two crêpes on each serving plate—spoon serving of roasted vegetables on each crêpe with three roasted asparagus spears protruding out one end. Roll up each crêpe filled with vegetables and place seam-side down on plate. Spoon hot Parmesan Béchamel Sauce over crêpes. Place Parmesan Cookie Crisp upright between crêpes. Garnish with fresh herb—sprig of sage, basil, rosemary, or parsley.

THE DUKE MANSION

Pan-Fried North Carolina Brook Trout with Beurre Blanc Sauce

Yield: 4 servings

For the beurre blanc:

- 1 tsp olive oil
- 1 tsp minced shallots
- 1 cup white wine
- 1 tsp fresh lime juice
- ¾ cup small green zebra tomatoes, diced, peeled, seeded
- 1 stick butter, cut into pieces (as needed)

For the trout:

- 1 cup all-purpose flour
- 1 tsp chopped parsley
  Kosher salt and black pepper, to taste
  Dash of cayenne pepper
  Dash of granulated garlic
- 2 butterflied brook or rainbow trout, split
- ½ stick butter
  Sweet potato, artichoke & crawfish hash, for serving (see page 61)

For the beurre blanc: Heat oil in a small skillet over medium heat. Add shallots and cook until soft. Add wine and lime juice. Bring to a boil, then lower heat and simmer until reduced by half. Add tomatoes and enough butter to form a sauce thick enough to coat a spoon. Keep warm.

For the trout: Preheat oven to 350°F. In a bowl, combine flour, parsley, salt, pepper, cayenne, and granulated garlic. Dredge trout in flour mixture. Melt butter in a large, oven-proof skillet over medium heat. Add trout to skillet, flesh-side-down, and cook until lightly browned. Turn trout, transfer skillet to the oven and bake for 4 minutes.

To serve: Fill a ⅓ cup measure with sweet potato hash and invert over center of a plate. Cut a trout fillet in half crossways and arrange on top of hash. Drizzle beurre blanc around outside of plate and serve.

Rosemary House B&B

Pappardelle with Roasted Winter Squash, Arugula, and Pine Nuts

Yield: 4 servings

- 4 cups peeled butternut squash, (1-inch) cubed
- 2 Tbsp balsamic vinegar
- 2 tsp olive oil
- ½ tsp salt, divided
- 8 oz. uncooked pappardelle (wide ribbon pasta) or fettuccine
- 1 Tbsp butter
- ¼ cup pine nuts
- 1 Tbsp chopped fresh sage
- 2 garlic cloves, minced
- 2 cups trimmed arugula
- ½ cup (4-oz.) grated fresh Asiago cheese
- ½ tsp coarsely ground black pepper

Preheat oven to 475°F. Combine squash, vinegar, oil, and ¼ teaspoon salt in a large bowl; toss well to coat. Arrange squash mixture in a single layer on a jelly-roll pan coated with cooking spray. Bake for 25 minutes or until tender and lightly browned, stirring occasionally. While squash bakes, cook pasta according to the package directions, omitting salt and fat. Drain in a colander over a bowl, reserving 2 tablespoons cooking liquid. Melt butter in a large nonstick skillet over medium heat. Add pine nuts, sage, and garlic; cook 3 minutes or just until the pine nuts begin to brown, stirring occasionally. Place pasta, reserved cooking liquid, pine nut mixture, and squash mixture in a large bowl; toss gently to combine. Add remaining ¼ teaspoon of salt, and the arugula, cheese, and black pepper; toss gently to combine. Serve immediately.

Beaufort House Inn

Roasted Butternut Squash & Goat Cheese Turnover with a Mango/Maple Glaze

Yield: 8 servings

¼ cup mango nectar juice
¼ cup maple syrup
2 cups butternut squash, roasted, mashed
1 cup goat cheese, crumbled
1 pkg. puff pastry sheets
1 egg – for egg wash
   Dried basil flakes

Preheat oven to 400°F. In a saucepan, heat the mango nectar and maple syrup for glaze. Set aside until serving. Roast 1 large butternut squash in the oven. Scoop out roasted butternut pulp; mash pulp and reserve until final baking time—can be done up to 2 days before serving and held over in the refrigerator. Crumble goat cheese and have ready for preparation and baking.

Fold out 1 sheet of puff pastry on a floured board and cut into 4 equal squares. Brush all sides of each square of puff pastry with egg wash (egg mixed with small amount of water or milk). Place 2 Tbsp roasted butternut squash, goat cheese and dried basil crosswise—corner to corner—in each puff pastry square. Fold over puff pastry and pinch all around with a fork to secure. Make two scissor cuts in top of each turnover to let steam escape. Brush all over with egg wash. Repeat assembly with second puff pastry sheet. Place turnovers on parchment-lined baking sheet. Bake for 15–20 minutes, until golden brown and puffy. Remove from oven, place on individual serving plates, brush with warm Mango/Maple Glaze, sprinkle with dried basil, and serve immediately.

Fuquay Mineral Spring Inn

Sautéed Shrimp with Garlic, Fennel, Tomatoes and Orzo

Yield: 4 servings

- 3 Tbsp olive oil
- ½ lb. large shrimp, peeled and deveined
- 1 large fennel bulb with fronds, trimmed, thinly sliced, fronds reserved
- 2 Tbsp chopped garlic
- ½ tsp dried crushed red pepper
- 1 lb. plum tomatoes, chopped
- ⅓ cup dry white wine
- ¼ cup fresh lemon juice
- 20 kalamata olives or other brine-cured black olives, pitted, halved
- 1 cup (about 4 oz.), crumbled soft fresh goat cheese
- 3½ cups freshly cooked orzo (rice-shaped pasta, about 1 cup uncooked)

Heat 2 tablespoons oil in a large skillet over medium high heat. Add shrimp and sauté until almost cooked through, about 2 minutes per side. Transfer to a bowl. Add 1 tablespoon oil to the same skillet. Add sliced fennel, garlic, and crushed red pepper and sauté for 3 minutes. Add tomatoes and wine, simmer until fennel is tender, about 4 minutes. Return shrimp to the skillet and add lemon juice and olives and simmer until shrimp are cooked through, about 2 minutes. Season with salt and pepper, add goat cheese and simmer until cheese begins to melt, about 30 seconds.

To serve: place orzo in a bowl, stir in shrimp mixture, garnish with fennel fronds.

Rosemary House B&B
Soft Polenta with Vegetable Bolognese

Yield: 6 servings

Polenta:
- 2 cups water, divided
- 1 cup polenta (corn meal)
- 1 tsp salt
- 2 cups vegetable stock
- ½ cup grated Parmesan cheese

Bolognese:
- 1 Tbsp extra-virgin olive oil
- 1 green bell pepper, chunked
- 1 yellow bell pepper, chunked
- 1 small zucchini, chunked
- 4 oz. cremini mushrooms
- 2 carrots, peeled, chunked
- 2 celery stalks, chunked
- 1 large yellow onion, chunked
- 3 garlic cloves, smashed
- 2 Tbsp tomato paste
- ½ cup dry red wine
- 1 (15-oz.) can tomato purée
- 2 tsp dried Italian herbs
- ½ tsp fennel seeds
- Crushed red pepper flakes
- salt and pepper
- grated cheese for garnish

First, prepare the polenta. In a small bowl, whisk together 1 cup water with the cornmeal and salt. In a saucepan, bring the remaining cup water and 2 cups stock to a boil. Stir the cornmeal mixture into the boiling water and continue to stir for about 10 minutes until polenta is very thick.

To make Bolognese: Heat a large saucepot over medium-high heat. Add olive oil. Add vegetables (in small batches) to the food processor. Pulse until they are minced but still chunky. Add vegetables to the pan with olive oil, stir and cook until all moisture is cooked out and begin to brown, about 10 minutes. Add tomato paste and wine. Simmer another 5 minutes. Add tomato purée and spices, stir and heat through. Taste and adjust seasonings. Mound the polenta on plates, make a well in the center and ladle on the sauce. Sprinkle with the grated cheese.

Inn on Main Street
Three-Bean Turkey Chipotle Chili

Yield: 20 servings

1–1.5 pounds lean ground turkey
    2 Tbsp canola oil
    1 large onion, chopped into half-inch chunks
    1 large jalapeño or serrano pepper, chopped fine
    1 medium bell pepper, diced
    1 carrot, chopped into half-inch chunks
    2 lbs. (2 medium cans) tomatoes
    2 lbs. cannellini (white kidney) beans
    2 lbs. black beans
    2 lbs. red kidney beans
    1 Tbsp dried oregano
    1 Tbsp dried basil
    1 Tbsp chili powder
    1 Tbsp chipotle powder

In a large pan, brown turkey in canola oil on medium high heat. Add onion, peppers, and carrot. The carrot adds color and nutrition without really affecting the taste. Add tomatoes and beans to a 4 quart or larger slow cooker. Pour in meat and sautéed vegetables. Stir in spices and set on low for two or more hours.

Garnish individual bowls with corn tortilla strips, shredded cheese, and fresh cilantro, if desired.

Tips: Remove seeds from the jalapeño or serrano pepper before chopping if you prefer milder chili. Substitute tofu for turkey to make vegan chili.

Fruit Specialties

1889 WhiteGate Inn & Cottage

Baked Apples & Cranberries

Yield: 8 servings

8 apples, cored but not peeled
1 can whole berry cranberry sauce

Cut apples into bite-sized pieces and place in a medium baking dish that has been sprayed with cooking spray. Add the cranberry sauce and cover tightly with plastic wrap and bake in microwave on high for 20 minutes. Serve warm.

Big Mill B&B
Blueberry–Blackberry Jam

Yield: 4 pints plus some for tasting

"Fresh-picked berries, with some of the berries not totally ripe, make the best jam. So if you are able to pick your own and make the jam immediately, it will be worth it. My blueberries and blackberries are growing here on the farm, so they are very fresh. This jam is so gorgeous I almost hate to eat it."—Innkeeper

2 pints blueberries
2 pints blackberries
1 Tbsp lemon juice
7 cups sugar
½ tsp butter, to reduce foaming (optional)
6 oz. (2 pouches) liquid fruit pectin (Be sure to check expiration date)

Put half of the berries in a large enamel or stainless cooking pot and crush the berries, making juice. Stir in the remaining berries and lemon juice. Add the sugar and butter and bring to a full rolling boil that cannot be stirred down. Pay careful attention to the pot. It will boil over in a heartbeat and you don't know what a mess is until you boil over jam. While the berries are seriously boiling, quickly add the fruit pectin and stir for *exactly* one minute. Remove from heat and pour into sterilized jars, following canning directions. Seal and process according to canning instructions.

Tip: Don't double the recipe … I don't know why, but it will fail. If Irma in *The Joy of Cooking* says, "Don't double the recipe" then I won't even try it.

Note: Fresh blackberries are always good, but they ripen before my blueberries, so I freeze them for this jam.

CAROLINA B&B

Cantaloupe with Raspberry Coulis and Mascarpone

Yield: 8 servings

For the Coulis:

2	pints fresh raspberries
3	Tbsp honey
1	tsp fresh lemon juice
	Pinch of ginger

1	ripe cantaloupe
1	pint blueberries
	Chopped fresh mint
½	cup mascarpone cheese

Prepare the raspberry coulis by combining the raspberries, honey, lemon juice, and ginger in the bowl of a food processor. Pulse until smooth. Strain the mixture through a sieve and throw out the seeds left behind. Chill eight hours or overnight.

Cut the melon in half, remove the seeds and rind, and slice into 18–24 slices. Chill. To assemble the salad: Make a swoosh of mascarpone cheese on one end of the serving plates using about 1 tablespoon of mascarpone per serving. Arranging 2–3 melon slices on top in a fan shape. Spoon 1–2 tablespoons of the coulis over the melon and dust lightly with freshly chopped mint leaves.

BILTMORE VILLAGE INN
Caribbean Pears

Yield: 8 servings

"This dish always gets a lively reaction from guests."—Innkeeper

4 pears, peeled, halved, and cored
½ stick butter
1 cup packed brown sugar
1 cup orange juice
1 tsp coconut extract
3 cinnamon sticks, broken into "pear stem" lengths
1 kiwi, peeled, halved lengthwise and sliced

Preheat oven to 350°F. Put pears cut-side-down in a 7x11-inch baking dish. Heat butter and brown sugar in a saucepan over medium-low heat until melted and combined. Stir in orange juice and coconut extract. Bring mixture to a low boil, then pour over pears. Bake pears for 30 minutes.

Place 1 pear half on each plate. Pour a little pan sauce over each pear. Put a piece of cinnamon stick at the tip of each pear as a "stem," arrange kiwi around "stem" as "leaves" and serve.

The Ivy B&B

Cinnamon Baked Grapefruit

Yield: 2 servings

1   Ruby Red or Pink Grapefruit
1   tsp butter per half grapefruit
    cinnamon and sugar mixture
    cherries

Preheat oven to 350°F. Cut the grapefruit in half and score each section. Sprinkle the scored grapefruit with the cinnamon and sugar. Place the butter in the center of the grapefruit. Place a cherry in the center of the grapefruit. Place on foil-lined baking sheet or for two you can use toaster oven. Bake for 15 minutes. Let the baked grapefruit sit for 5 to 10 minutes before serving.

OLD NORTH DURHAM INN
Citrus Party Punch

Yield: 90 (4-oz.) servings

   8 cups water
   1 16-oz. can frozen orange juice concentrate
   1 12-oz. can frozen lemonade concentrate
   2 46-oz. cans unsweetened pineapple juice
2½ cups sugar
   ¼ cup lime juice
   2 2-liter bottles ginger ale, chilled
   2 1-liter bottles club soda, chilled
      Sliced oranges, limes, lemons for garnish
      Ice cubes

Make the following juice mixture ahead of time and chill until ready to serve. This is a lot of liquid, so you'll need to make it in your largest bowl or pot—fills 2 large punch bowls. Combine water and the frozen concentrates and stir to dissolve. Stir in pineapple juice, sugar, and lime juice, and stir to dissolve sugar. Chill.

To serve, pour half of the punch mixture into a large punch bowl. Slowly pour in 1 bottle of ginger ale and 1 bottle of club soda. Stir gently to mix. Add ice until punch bowl is full. Garnish with fruit slices, if desired.

Repeat with remaining punch mixture when needed, or freeze for next party.

Carolina B&B
Deconstructed Ambrosia Salad

Yield: 4 servings

1 large pink grapefruit	2–3 Tbsp pomegranate seeds OR 2–3 Tbsp dried cranberries
1 large white grapefruit	
1 blood orange	
1 navel orange	Chopped fresh mint
2 Clementine oranges	2 tsp good honey
¼ cup blueberries	2–3 Tbsp homemade marshmallow fluff (recipe follows)
2 Tbsp sliced almonds	

Using a knife, remove all of the rind and pith from the citrus fruits. Slice each one carefully into at least four good slices. Arrange them artfully on a plate, then sprinkle with blueberries, almonds, pomegranite seeds and mint. Drizzle some honey sparingly over the arranged fruit. Just before serving, place about 1–2 teaspoons of marshmallow fluff in the center of the salad and then, using a kitchen torch, toast the fluff to a light brown. It is important to use homemade fluff, as commercial varieties contain preservatives which inhibit the fluff from browning. It will go directly to burnt!

Marshmallow Fluff

3 egg whites	½ tsp salt
2 cups light corn syrup	2 cups powdered sugar
	1 Tbsp vanilla extract

In a large mixing bowl combine egg whites, corn syrup and salt. Beat with mixer on high for 10 minutes. Mixture will increase about three times in volume and become quite thick. On low speed, add the powdered sugar. Stir in the vanilla extract until well blended.

This recipe makes about four cups of fluff but it freezes and defrosts easily. Measure it into smaller containers and use it as needed.

THE IVY B&B

Fried Cinnamon Apples

Yield: 6 servings

6	medium apples
¼	stick butter
½	cup brown sugar
¼	tsp cinnamon
1	Tbsp sugar
	apple pie spice
¼	cup orange juice (optional)

Peel, core and slice the apples. Melt butter in a small skillet. Add apples once skillet is hot. Sprinkle the cinnamon/sugar and brown sugar over the apples. Shake a small amount of apple pie spice on each apple slice. If the apples are not very juicy, add the orange juice. Simmer until tender, stirring occasionally, approximately 15 minutes.

Tip: As a variation, you can add some flavored syrup such as caramel.

Pamlico House B&B
Honey Vanilla Yogurt

Yield: 10–12 servings

4 cups plain yogurt
¼ cup honey
1 tsp vanilla

Mix the three ingredients well. Serve over your favorite seasonal fruit—I usually serve it over papaya.

The papaya tree is a horticultural wonder, growing from seed to a 20-foot, fruit-bearing tree in less than 18 months. Slightly green papayas will ripen quickly at room temperature, especially if placed in a paper bag. Papaya is a very good source of vitamins A and C.

THE LAMPLIGHT INN
Icey Fruit Treat

Yield: 6–8 servings

*"A friend shared this recipe with me and the guests love it.
It's great to keep on hand in the freezer."*—Innkeeper

3	ripe bananas, mashed
1	cup sugar
6–8	Tbsp lemon juice
1	small can crushed pineapple
¾–1	cup orange juice

Mix and freeze. Serve slushy with fresh berries on top.

Home Coming Bed and Breakfast

Mama Hazel's Fruit Salad

Yield: 10 servings

"Deborah's grandmother, Mama Hazel, selflessly cared for family her entire life. She brought this recipe home from work one day and it has remained in the family for over 50 years. It was served at Mama Hazel's memorial service, a loving tribute to a woman who was close to her Lord Jesus."—Innkeeper

- 1 can mandarin oranges
- 1 can crushed pineapple in its own juice (tidbits also o.k.)
- 1 small can or bag coconut
- 1 container sour cream
- 1 small bag miniature marshmallows

Mix all ingredients together, add marshmallows as needed (for sweeter add more marshmallows). Refrigerate. Serve cold.

At Cumberland Falls Bed and Breakfast Inn

Pastry Cream

Yield: approximately 3½ cups

"Excellent for use in fruit parfaits."—Innkeeper

    1   cup whole milk, divided
    5   Tbsp granulated sugar, divided
    4   large egg yolks
 2½   Tbsp cornstarch
    6   oz. cream cheese (room temperature)
  ¼   cup plus 2 Tbsp fresh lemon juice
    1   tsp finely grated lemon zest plus extra strips for garnish
    1   whole vanilla bean, scraped
    1   cup heavy cream

In a medium saucepan bring ¾ cup milk to a boil with 3 tablespoons sugar. Remove from heat. In a medium bowl whisk the egg yolks with the cornstarch and the rest of the milk plus 2 tablespoons of sugar. Gradually whisk the hot milk into the egg yolks then return the mixture to the saucepan, whisking constantly over medium heat until thickening occurs. Lower the heat adding the cream cheese, lemon juice, zest and vanilla until completely smooth. Place in a bowl and press a piece of plastic wrap directly onto the surface of the custard and chill two hours.

At Cumberland Falls Bed and Breakfast Inn

Peaches n' Cream

Yield: 1 serving

"This is used as a fruit dish. To say guests 'lap it up' is an understatement of its reception! Simply multiply the recipe as needed for the given number of guests."—Innkeeper

1	large ripe fresh peach, peeled, cut in half and pitted
½	Tbsp butter
2	tsp heavy cream
2	tsp white Zinfandel or other fruity white wine
½	tsp vanilla extract
1	Tbsp packed brown sugar
	Pinch of cinnamon
	Whipped cream, for serving

Preheat oven to 350°F. Clean peach cavity with a fruit baller. Place peach halves in a small baking dish. Put butter in cavity of each peach half. Add cream. Sprinkle wine over peach, letting some accumulate in bottom of dish. Sprinkle vanilla and brown sugar over peach. Sprinkle lightly with cinnamon. Bake for 20–30 minutes, until tender and bubbly. Serve with a dollop of whipped cream.

THE KING'S DAUGHTERS INN
Pear-spiked Applesauce

Yield: 4 servings

4 McIntosh apples, peeled, quartered, and cored
2 Bartlett pears, peeled, quartered, and cored
1 cup water
1 Tbsp lemon juice
1 tsp sugar
¼ tsp cinnamon

In a large, heavy saucepan, bring the apples, pears, water, and lemon juice to a boil. Reduce the heat and simmer until the fruit breaks down to a thick, chunky purée, about 30–50 minutes. Remove from heat and stir in the sugar and cinnamon, if necessary (taste first!).

Serve warm or chilled.

Tips: You can use different kinds of apples but may need to adjust the amount of sugar or lemon juice. If they're really ripe, you can use less water. Also, you can use a cinnamon stick during the cooking process instead of cinnamon after the fact.

Andon-Reid Inn B&B
Poached Peaches with Lemon Cheese Mousse

Yield: 12 servings

3 cups water
1½ cups sugar
⅓ cup lemon juice
1 Tbsp vanilla
6 medium peaches, halved and pitted
Fresh raspberries

Combine first 4 ingredients in large glass bowl. Microwave on high for 10 minutes. Stir until sugar dissolves. Add peach halves to syrup and microwave on high for 4 minutes. Refrigerate covered overnight.

½ cup ricotta cheese
¼ cup cream cheese
3 Tbsp confectioners' sugar
1½ tsp lemon rind
½ tsp vanilla

In a bowl, beat all ingredients together, cover and refrigerate.

To serve: place peach halves on serving plate cut side up. Spoon mousse into pit cavity and sprinkle with nutmeg. Place a couple of fresh raspberries on each plate.

The Ivy B&B
Warm Fruit Compote

Yield: 4 servings

- ¼ cup chopped walnuts or pecans
- 1 jar Dole Tropical Fruit
- 3 Tbsp brown sugar
- ¼ cup golden raisins (optional)
- 1 banana

Roast the nuts in a skillet, then set aside. Drain a small amount of juice from the fruit into a separate skillet. Heat the juice and brown sugar until it begins to thicken. Add the fruit and golden raisins. Heat well. Add the nuts and banana slices last, just before serving.

About half of the world's raisin supply comes from California. Dark raisins are sun-dried for several weeks, thereby producing their shriveled appearance and dark color. Golden raisins are treated with sulpher dioxide to prevent their color from darkening, and dried with artificial heat.

BIG MILL B&B
Watermelon Punch

Yield: 20 servings

"Summertime and watermelons just go together. When I was growing up on the farm my father had three rows of watermelons that were at least a city block long. In July and August we would drive the pickup truck into the field and load all the watermelons into the truck bed. We brought them back to the house and laid them in the shade of the pecan trees. Every afternoon, we would stop work and come and cut a watermelon, eat what we wanted and then take the remains to the cows and the mules."—Innkeeper

- 1 lemon (an orange may be substituted)
- 1 (2-liter) bottle lemon-lime soda, divided
- 1 large watermelon, chilled
- 1 (6-oz.) can frozen orange juice concentrate
- ¾ cup sugar or to taste

Slice the lemon crosswise and arrange in a circular ring mold pan. Fill with one liter of the lemon-lime soda. Freeze.

Cut watermelon into halves. Scoop out pulp and place in blender, seeds and all. Blend for several seconds on medium speed. Strain through a fine sieve colander, squeezing out juice. Place watermelon juice in large container with lid. Add orange juice concentrate and sugar and stir until sugar and orange juice are dissolved. Chill until ready to serve.

When ready to serve, pour watermelon mixture into a clear glass or plastic punch bowl. Add the remaining liter of lemon-lime soda and stir. Place ice ring in the punch bowl and serve.

Tip: This punch is a gorgeous red, so be sure to serve it in a clear glass or plastic container.

Desserts

Beaufort House Inn
Apple Raisin Bread Pudding

Yield: 6 one-cup ramekin servings

6	large croissants
⅛	cup Madeira
¼	cup golden raisins
½	tsp cinnamon
½	tsp ground nutmeg
2	Tbsp melted butter
¾	cup chopped apple—Gala, skin on
4	large eggs (organic best)
¾	cup white sugar
1½	cups heavy whipping cream
1	Tbsp vanilla

Preheat oven to 350°F. Break croissants into 1–2-inch pieces and set aside. Heat the Madeira gently and add raisins to plump. Remove from heat and set aside for 10 minutes. In a bowl, stir cinnamon and ground nutmeg into chopped apples until coated and set aside. Butter bottom and sides of 6 ramekins. Alternate layers of apple mixture, half of the croissant chunks, raisins, and remaining apples, and end with remaining croissants on top. Whisk together eggs and sugar until frothy. Whisk in cream and vanilla. Press down lightly on croissant layers in ramekins. Pour egg mixture slowly over croissant layers. Let bread pudding sit for 5 minutes before beginning to bake. Bake for 1 hour. Serve with a light dusting of powdered sugar, and with warm maple syrup on the side.

FUQUAY MINERAL SPRING INN
Caribbean Crème Brûlée

Yield: 6 servings

- 1 cup heavy cream
- 1 cup fresh or canned coconut milk
- 8 egg yolks
- ⅓ cup plus 12 tsp sugar
- 1 tsp vanilla extract
- ½ cup dark rum
- 3 Tbsp sweetened flaked coconut, toasted

Preheat oven to 300°F. In a large bowl, combine cream, coconut milk, egg yolks, ⅓ cup of sugar, vanilla, and rum; whisk until smooth (skim any foam or bubbles that may appear). Divide mixture among 6 individual ramekins or ovenproof custard cups. Place ramekins in a baking pan filled with 1-inch of hot water. Bake about for 40–50 minutes, until set around edges, but still a little loose in center. Remove from oven and let ramekins cool to room temperature in water bath. Remove ramekins from water bath and chill for at least 2 hours.

When ready to serve, sprinkle about 2 teaspoons of sugar over each crème brûlée. With a kitchen torch or under a preheated broiler, brown tops of crème brûlées until sugar has hardened (if using a kitchen torch, be careful as this custard contains alcohol which could cause the sugar to spatter from the flame). Sprinkle toasted coconut over crème brûlées and serve.

Beaufort House Inn
Mocha Café Au Lait

Yield: 8 (½ cup) servings

2½ cups half & half cream
⅓ cup all-purpose flour
⅛ tsp salt
1 (14-oz.) can sweetened condensed milk
2 egg yolks
2 Tbsp instant coffee granules
1 Tbsp Swiss Miss hot chocolate mix
1 Tbsp. vanilla, good quality
¾ cup whipping cream (no sugar added)
   freshly grated nutmeg
   mint sprigs

Gently heat cream in a heavy deep saucepan until barely frothing around edges. Gradually whisk in all-purpose flour and salt until well blended and smooth.

Add next 4 ingredients, whisking constantly for 12–20 minutes on medium/low heat until custard thickens. Remove from heat and stir in good quality vanilla.

Remove from heat when adequately thickened and set in a cool place. Continue to whisk every few minutes to let steam heat release. When custard is "set," serve immediately by spooning into ½ cup ramekins and garnishing with dollop of fresh whipped cream, grated nutmeg, and mint sprig.

ANDON-REID INN B&B
Pumpkin Tiramisu

Yield: 10–12 servings

   2 cups chilled whipped cream
   1 cup sugar
   1 (8-oz.) container mascarpone cheese
   1 (15-oz.) can pure pumpkin
1¼ tsp pumpkin pie spice
   2 (3-oz.) pkgs. halved ladyfingers
   ¼ cup Grand Marnier, divided
   3 oz. crushed gingersnap cookies, divided

Plan ahead—needs overnight refrigeration.

Beat whipping cream and sugar until peaks form. Set aside. In a bowl, mix the mascarpone cheese, pumpkin, and spice. Beat until filling is smooth, then fold in whipped cream. Line the bottom of a 9-inch springform pan with one package of ladyfingers, overlapping and crowding to fit. Use pastry brush and brush the ladyfingers with 2 table-spoons of Grand Marnier. Spread half of the filling over the ladyfingers. Sprinkle half of the gingersnaps over filling. Repeat with second pack-age of ladyfingers, remaining 2 tablespoons Grand Marnier, remain-ing filling and gingersnaps. Wrap tightly with plastic, then foil. Chill overnight. To unmold, run knife around inside edge of pan. Release pan sides; sprinkle with gingersnap cookies.

1906 Pine Crest Inn
Banana Pudding Napoleon

Yield: 6 servings

Wafers:
- 7 oz. all-purpose flour
- ¾ tsp aluminum free baking powder
- ½ tsp kosher salt
- 4 oz. unsalted butter, room temperature
- 3½ oz vanilla sugar
- 1 large egg
- 4 tsp vanilla extract
- 1 Tbsp whole milk

Custard Mousse:
- 2 cups heavy cream
- 1 vanilla bean, scraped

- 6 eggs, separated
- ⅔ cup superfine sugar, separated
- ¼ cup cornstarch
- ¼ tsp salt
- ½ tsp cream of tartar

Meringue:
- 3 egg whites, room temperature
- 1 tsp cream of tartar
- 2 Tbsp superfine sugar

4–5 ripe bananas

Position one oven rack in the top third of the oven and another in the bottom third. Heat the oven to 350°F. Sift together the flour, baking powder, and salt in a small bowl and set aside. Cream the butter and vanilla sugar in the bowl of a stand mixer on medium speed for 2 minutes, stopping to scrape down the sides of the bowl after 1 minute. Add the egg and incorporate on medium speed for 30 seconds. Scrape down the sides of the mixer bowl. Add the vanilla extract and milk and blend on low speed for 15 seconds. Add the flour mixture and mix on low speed just to incorporate. Chill the batter in the refrigerator for at least 10 minutes before scooping.

Scoop the batter in 2-inch balls and arrange them on parchment-lined half sheet pans, approximately 8–10 cookies per pan. Use the heel of your hand to slightly flatten each ball. Bake, 2 pans at a time, rotating the pans halfway through the baking, until golden brown, about 15 to 20 minutes. Remove the pans to a cooling rack to cool completely before removing the cookies from the pan.

To prepare the mousse, scald the cream, vanilla seeds and vanilla pod in a heavy saucepan. Remove from heat, remove vanilla pod and set aside to cool slightly. Meanwhile, beat egg yolks and 1/3 cup sugar in a bowl until the mixture is creamy and pale yellow, and the mixture leaves a "ribbon trail" when the whisk/beaters are lifted. Beat in the cornstarch.

Slowly add a ladle of the hot cream mixture to the beaten yolks, whisking constantly, to bring them to temperature, then slowly pour the yolk mixture into the pot with the remaining hot cream, still beating constantly. Return pot to medium heat, whisking constantly (it will thicken as it reaches a boil). Reduce the heat to low and continue to cook for 2 minutes more, stirring constantly. Remove from heat and strain into a cold bowl.

In a clean bowl, whip egg whites with cream of tartar and the 2 tablespoons of superfine sugar until stiff peaks form. Fold half the whites in the custard mixture to lighten it, then scrape the remaining whites in and gently but quickly fold them in until well mixed but not deflated. Place in Piping bag, no tip is necessary. Chill before compiling Napoleon.

Assembly: Using 3–4 inch ring molds or free-form, place a wafer on the bottom of a plate or sheet pan. Pipe a layer of custard and then top with sliced bananas. Add another wafer and repeat to create second layer. Pipe additional custard on top of bananas and place third wafer on top. Chill for at least 6 hours.

When ready to serve, pipe meringue on top, making sure to leave small, decorative peaks. Use a kitchen torch to lightly brulée the meringue. Drizzle with caramel or rum syrup and serve.

Carolina B&B
Upside Down Mango Bread Pudding

Yield: 6 servings

- 1 stick butter (½ cup)
- 1 cup packed brown sugar
- 2 Tbsp dark corn syrup
- 6 Champagne Mangos
    large loaf of good bread (with a density like a homemade loaf)

The night before serving:

Melt together butter, brown sugar, and corn syrup over medium heat and stir until smooth. Grease 6 (1-cup) ramekins. Divide sauce equally among the ramekins. Cut in half and use a big spoon to scoop out the inside of mangos. Arrange the pieces in the bottom of the ramekins on top of the sauce. Cut a large loaf of good bread into 2-inch cubes. Fit the cubes into the ramekins on top of the fruit, squeezing to fit.

In a large bowl, whisk together:

- 5–6 large eggs
- 1½ cups half & half
- 1 tsp vanilla
- 1–2 tsp Grand Marnier
    dash of salt

Pour the egg mixture equally over the bread, trying to moisten all of it. Cover and place in the refrigerator overnight.

Preheat oven to 350°F. Bake puddings uncovered in middle of the oven until puffed and the edges are pale golden (about 35–40 minutes). Remove from oven and let rest for five minutes. Place a plate on top of the ramekin and invert. Be careful—the syrup is quite hot! Lift off the ramekin and serve.

Biltmore Village Inn
Cold Oven Pound Cake

Yield: 1 Cake

"This pound cake has a wonderful texture and a delightful, sugary crust. Plan ahead, it should sit for a day before slicing. This cake freezes beautifully."—Innkeeper

2	sticks butter, softened
½	cup vegetable oil
4	eggs
3	cups all-purpose flour
¼	tsp salt
3	cups sugar
1	cup milk
½	tsp rum extract
1	tsp vanilla extract
1	tsp lemon extract

Grease a large tube cake pan. In a large bowl, beat butter and oil until smooth. Add eggs, 1 at a time, beating well after each addition. In a medium bowl, combine flour, salt, and sugar. Add flour mixture and milk alternately to butter mixture, mixing well after each addition. Add rum, vanilla and lemon extracts; mix well. Pour batter into pan. Place pan in a cold oven. Turn oven temperature to 350°F and bake for 90 minutes.

Variations: Soak 1 cup of raisins in ½ cup of brandy, drain and toss with ½ cup flour. Stir raisins into batter last. Add your favorite nuts with, or instead of, the raisins.

THE COVE B&B
Ocracoke Fig Cake

Yield: 16 servings

3 eggs
1½ cups sugar
1 cup salad oil
2 cups flour
1 tsp nutmeg
1 tsp cinnamon
1 tsp salt
1 tsp allspice
½ cup buttermilk
1 tsp vanilla
1 tsp soda, dissolved in a little hot water
1 cup fig preserves (chopped)/can substitute with dates
1 cup chopped nuts

Preheat oven to 350°F. In a bowl, beat 3 eggs, add sugar and oil. In a separate bowl, sift together the dry ingredients, then add to egg mixture alternating with buttermilk. Add vanilla and soda and fold in figs and nuts. Pour into well-greased tube pan and bake for about an hour.

Morehead Manor B&B
Orange Pecan Spiced Pound Cake

Yield: 6-8 servings

- 2 cups pecans, toasted, finely chopped and divided
- 1 stick of butter at room temperature
- 1 cup granulated white sugar
- 3 eggs
- 2/3 cup water
- 1 cup all-purpose flour
- 1 box butter flavored cake mix
- 8 oz. sour cream
- 2 tsp ground cinnamon
- 1 tsp ground nutmeg
- ½ tsp ground cloves
- 1 tsp each – vanilla, lemon and orange extracts
- 2 Tbsp grated orange rind

Preheat oven to 350°F. Generously butter (1–2 Tbsp) a 10-inch tube pan. Sprinkle 1¼ cups finely chopped pecans in tube pan. Shake evenly to coat bottom, sides, and tube of pan. Make certain that remaining nuts are evenly distributed in the bottom of the pan. Set aside. In a large mixing bowl, cream butter and sugar. Add eggs, one at a time. Gradually add water, flour, cake mix, sour cream, spices, extracts, orange rind, and remaining pecans. Bake for 1 hour or until done.

Home Coming Bed & Breakfast

Sam's Coconut Cake

Yield: 10 servings

"This was a special cake baked every Christmas for Sam by his grandmother, Granny Dot, who affectionately called Sam 'Spoiled Rotten.'"—Innkeeper

  1 box Duncan Hines Golden Butter Recipe cake mix
1½ cups water
  2 cups sugar, divided
 12 oz. sour cream
  3 packs frozen coconut

Plan ahead—needs overnight refrigeration.

Follow the instructions on the cake box for a one layer oblong pan. Let it cool. Boil water and a cup of sugar until sugar is dissolved. Poke holes in the cake and pour over the sugar mixture. Mix sour cream, a cup of sugar, and frozen coconut and frost the top of the cake. Refrigerate for 1 day before serving.

Glade Valley B&B
Chocolate Chip Cookies

Yield: 3 dozen

¾ cup butter-flavored shortening
1¼ cups firmly packed light brown sugar
2 Tbsp milk
1 Tbsp vanilla
1 egg
1¾ cups all-purpose flour
1 tsp salt
¾ tsp baking soda
1½ cups semi-sweet chocolate chips

Preheat oven to 375ºF. Combine butter-flavored shortening, light brown sugar, milk, and vanilla in large bowl. Beat at medium speed until well blended. Beat egg into creamed mixture. In a separate bowl, combine flour, salt, and baking soda. Mix into creamed mixture just until blended. Stir in chocolate chips. Drop rounded tablespoonfuls of dough 3 inches apart onto ungreased baking sheet. Bake for 8 to 10 minutes.

The Inn on Mill Creek
Chewy Mint Chocolate Chip Cookies

Yield: 4 dozen cookies

Cookie Ingredients
- 1¼ cups butter, softened
- 1½ cups sugar
- 2 eggs
- 1½ tsp vanilla extract
- ½ tsp peppermint extract
- 2 cups all-purpose flour
- ¾ cups unsweetened cocoa powder
- 1 tsp baking soda
- ½ tsp salt
- 1 cup semi-sweet chocolate chips

Frosting Ingredients
- 1 cup powdered sugar
- 2 Tbsp butter, softened
- 1 Tbsp milk
- ¼ tsp peppermint extract
- 1 drop green food coloring

In a large mixing bowl, cream butter and sugar until light and fluffy. Beat in eggs, one at a time. Stir in vanilla and peppermint extracts. In a large bowl, sift together flour, cocoa powder, baking soda, and salt. Add dry ingredient mixture into butter/egg/sugar mixture and mix well. Stir in chocolate chips with a spoon. Place dough in refrigerator and cool for 30 minutes.

Preheat oven to 350°F. Roll dough into 1-inch balls and place on ungreased cookie sheet; flatten with glass or back of spoon. Bake 8–10 minutes; cookies will be soft when removed from oven. Cool for 5 minutes on sheet; transfer to wire racks to finish cooling.

Mix frosting ingredients together (adding additional teaspoon of milk will make thinner icing if desired). Frost cookies and cool in refrigerator for 30 minutes to set frosting.

803 Elizabeth B&B
Toasted Coconut Cookies

Yield: 36 cookies

"This cookie recipe is from a friend in yoga class."—Innkeeper

- 1 cup sweetened flaked coconut
- 1 stick butter, softened
- ¾ cup sugar
- 1 large egg
- ½ tsp coconut or almond extract
- 1½ cups all-purpose flour
- ½ tsp baking soda
- 1 tsp baking powder
- ½ cup crispy rice cereal
- ½ cup old-fashioned rolled oats

Preheat oven to 350°F. Spread coconut on a baking sheet and toast lightly in oven for 7–10 minutes; remove from oven and cool.

In a large bowl, beat butter until fluffy. Gradually beat in sugar. Add egg and coconut or almond extract; beat well. In a medium bowl, combine flour, baking soda, and baking powder. Add flour mixture to butter mixture, a little at a time, beating well after each addition. Stir in coconut, crispy rice cereal, and oats.

Drop dough by heaping teaspoonsful onto a parchment paper-lined cookie sheet. (The cookie sheet can be greased instead, but parchment paper makes cookie baking much easier—no cookie sheets to wash!) Bake cookies for 12–15 minutes, until golden. Slide parchment paper off cookie sheet and let cookies cool.

Benjamin W. Best House
Pumpkin Bars

Yield: 10–12 servings

2 cups self-rising flour
2 tsp cinnamon
1 tsp baking soda
2 cups sugar
2 cups pumpkin
4 eggs
1 cup chopped nuts
1 cup vegtable oil

Frosting:

16 oz. powdered sugar
8 oz. pkg. cream cheese
2 tsp vanilla

Preheat oven to 350°F. In a bowl, combine first 8 ingredients. Pour into a greased and floured 12x10-inch pan. Bake for 25 minutes. Cool. Combine ingredients for frosting and frost.

Morehead Manor B&B
Blueberry Delight

Yield: 6–8 servings

"A yummy summertime dessert that's cool and light."—Innkeeper

Crust:

- 1 cup all-purpose flour
- ½ cup packed brown sugar
- 1 stick butter or margarine, melted
- 1 cup chopped pecans

Filling:

- 1 (8-oz.) pkg. cream cheese
- ¾ cup sugar
- 1 tsp vanilla extract
- 1 (9-oz.) container Cool Whip

Topping:

- 1 pint fresh blueberries (frozen can be used)
- 1 cup sugar
- 1 Tbsp cornstarch
- 1 tsp lemon juice

For the crust: Preheat oven to 350°F. Combine crust ingredients and pat over bottom of a 9x13-inch baking dish. Bake for 10–15 minutes, then remove from oven and cool thoroughly.

For the filling: Blend filling ingredients thoroughly and spread over crust.

For the topping: Mix blueberries and sugar in a medium saucepan over medium heat and bring to a boil. Mix cornstarch with a small amount of water until smooth, then stir into blueberry mixture. Stir in lemon juice. Lower heat and simmer until thickened. Cool, then pour over filling. Chill for at least 2 hours before serving.

Big Mill B&B
Fried Peach Jacks

Yield: 6–8 servings

"I remember eating fried peach jacks whenever I went to "Dinner on the Ground" at a small country church in eastern North Carolina. Dinner on the Ground all over the South celebrated the end of revival—they called it Homecoming. Like peach jacks, these celebrations are a fading tradition. And lard is making a comeback!!"—Innkeeper

Filling
- 1 (6-oz.) pkg. dried peaches*
- 1½–2 cups water
- 1 cup sugar

Dough
- 2 cups all-purpose flour
- 1 tsp salt
- ½ cup shortening
- ½ cup milk
- Extra flour for dusting cutting board and rolling pin

For Frying
- ½–1 cup lard (or canola oil)

Make filling the day before you cook the jacks. Simmer peaches and water in a small saucepan for 45 minutes to an hour until peaches are soft. Be careful, they tend to stick. Add water if needed. Add the sugar and cook 15 minutes more, stirring often. Remove from heat and refrigerate overnight. You will have 2½ cups cooked peaches.

(Continued next page)

Fried Peach Jacks *(Continued)*

In a bowl, stir together the flour and salt. Using two forks, cut in the shortening. Add milk and stir. Separate into 6 to 8 portions. Using the extra flour and a rolling pin, roll each dough piece into a 6-inch round. Roll dough as thin as you can without tearing dough.

Put 2 tablespoons cooked peaches in the center of the rolled dough. Fold the edges over to make a half circle. Crimp edges with a fork.

Melt lard in a medium-size frying pan. Grease should be quite hot before you fry the jacks. Fry jacks until they are golden in color. Turn and brown the other side. Remove from heat and drain on paper towels. Continue until all jacks are cooked. Best when served warm.

*Use dried fruit … in the South we use dried peaches, apples, or cherries. Fresh fruit just doesn't have the zing.

Morning Glory Inn
Lemon Chess Pie

Yield: 2 9-inch pies

6 Tbsp butter, melted
3 cups sugar
1 tsp salt
3 tsp lemon zest
3 lemons
6 large eggs
2 9-inch pie crusts

Preheat oven to 350°F and place large cookie sheet on center rack. Melt butter in a mixing bowl in microwave, 35 seconds; then 25 more seconds. Add sugar and salt to the butter and whisk together. Zest two of the lemons into the bowl for the 3 teaspoons of zest. Cut all three lemons in half and squeeze juice into bowl and whisk contents thoroughly. (May need to add additional few tablespoons lemon juice.) Add eggs to ingredients and whisk together for approximately 50 strokes. Pour evenly into two pie shells. Place pies on cookie sheet in oven and set timer to bake for 34 minutes. Pies are done when slightly brown and mostly set. Remove from oven and cool completely on wire racks. Keep refrigerated.

Beaufort House Inn
Fresh Lemon Cups with Strawberries
Yield: One 9-inch pie or 8 (½ cup) servings

"This recipe can be baked and served as we do at the Beaufort House Inn in individual ramekins with some fresh fruit on top, or it is enough to fill one 9-inch pie shell. When I make it in a pie shell, I serve it as a dessert with fresh strawberries or other fruit, usually soaked in a little Madeira or Marsala for a little while before serving."—Innkeeper

1¾ cups granulated sugar
1½ Tbsp yellow cornmeal
1¼ Tbsp all-purpose flour
6 eggs, beaten until frothy
½ cup half & half or heavy cream
6 tsp melted butter
1½ Tbsp fresh lemon zest, chopped fine
6 Tbsp fresh lemon juice
1 (9-inch) pie shell, optional

Preheat oven to 350°F. In a bowl, mix together granulated sugar, cornmeal, and all-purpose flour. Add beaten eggs, cream, butter, lemon zest, and lemon juice. Beat until smooth. Pour into either individual ramekins or pie shell. Bake approximately 30–40 minutes until golden brown on top and toothpick comes out clean. Top with fresh sliced strawberries and mint sprig. Serve warm.

Beaufort House Inn
Peach Buckle

Yield: 6–8 (1 cup) servings

Cake Layer:

1¾	cups sugar
½	cup butter
3	eggs
2¼	cups all-purpose flour
1	Tbsp baking powder
¾	tsp salt
¾	cup buttermilk
1	Tbsp vanilla extract

Combine sugar and butter in the bowl of a standard mixer. Beat with paddle attachment until light and fluffy. Add eggs one at a time, beating after each addition. In a separate bowl, sift together dry ingredients and add to the egg mixture alternately with buttermilk and vanilla.

Brown Sugar Topping:

½	cup packed light brown sugar
¾	cup all-purpose flour
2	Tbsp cold butter

Mix all ingredients together, mashing with a fork, until the butter is all incorporated into bits smaller than a pea. Refrigerate.

(Continued next page)

Peach Buckle *(Continued)*

Peach Filling:

4 cups peaches, cut into ½-inch chunks
   sugar to taste (optional)
1 Tbsp cornstarch with small amount of water
   (slurry: thickening agent)

In a medium saucepan, combine peaches with sugar, if desired. Let the fruit macerate for up to 15 minutes so that some of the natural juices start to release. Cook peaches over low heat until softened but not mushy. Add slurry slowly and stir to thicken slightly. Simmer for 10 minutes to ensure cornstarch is cooked off.

To Assemble:

Preheat oven to 400°F. Fill six or eight (8 oz.) ramekins less than half full with peach mixture. Top with equal portions of cake batter. Sprinkle each buckle with 2 tablespoons of brown sugar topping. Bake ramekins until cake batter is golden brown and set, about 15–20 minutes. Serve with a dollop of whipped cream or ice cream.

Tip: Other fruit may be substituted for fresh peaches.

A Bed of Roses, Victorian B&B
Peach Topped Bavarian Torte

Yield: 12 servings

"My sister Marianne gave me this recipe in 1972. I had to increase her original recipe to fit current springform pan sizes. It's a crowd pleaser. For the B&B, I cut it into squares to serve in the afternoons."—Innkeeper

Crust

- ¾ cup softened margarine or butter
- ½ cup sugar
- 3/8 tsp vanilla extract (we used Madagascar)
- 1 cup flour
- 1 cup finely chopped pecans

Cheesecake

- 12 oz. softened cream cheese
- 3/8 cup sugar
- 1½ eggs (not easy to do! I beat the second egg and pour in half)
- 1½ tsp vanilla

Topping

- 1 (29-oz.) can sliced cling peaches in juice, well drained
- 1 tsp cinnamon
- 1 tsp sugar

Preheat oven to 450°F. In a mixing bowl, beat margarine or butter with sugar and vanilla at medium speed until well blended. Add flour and mix. Stir in pecans. Flour your hands and press mixture into the bottom and 1 inch up the sides of a springform pan.

(Continued next page)

Peach Topped Bavarian Torte *(Continued)*

In a clean mixing bowl, beat cream cheese and sugar at medium speed until smooth. Beat in eggs and vanilla until blended. Pour into spring-form pan.

In large bowl combine cinnamon and sugar. Add peaches and toss lightly. Arrange peaches on top of cream cheese mixture and bake 10 minutes. Reduce heat to 400°F and continue baking 25 minutes more. Cool in pan for 20 minutes, then carefully remove sides. Serve warm or refrigerate.

Beaufort House Inn
Pear Dumpling with Blueberry Sauce

Yield: 4 servings

1 Pillsbury pastry pie round
1 egg white
4 pear halves, drained
   nutmeg
   raw sugar
   Smuckers Blueberry Syrup
   powdered sugar

Preheat convection oven to 400°F. Spray a baking sheet with nonstick spray to ensure no sticking. Cut pastry round into 4 equal parts. Brush all inside edges with egg wash (egg white and water mix) for best seal. Place one pear half in middle of each pastry quarter— small end inward—and sprinkle lightly with ground nutmeg. Create dumpling shape by folding/pinching pastry around pear half—final shape is like a puffy triangle. Place on baking sheet and egg wash pastry all over outside of dumpling. Sprinkle liberally with raw sugar.

Bake for 15–18 minutes, then lower to 375°F if starting to burn on edges. Pastry should be glistening but dry to touch when done. Err on side of over baking just a little—undercooked pastry will be too doughy to serve.

To Serve: Puddle blueberry syrup in middle of mid-size plate. Place dumpling in center of syrup and sprinkle with powdered sugar. Add sprinkle of fresh blueberries if desired. Serve immediately and warn guests that dumpling is HOT in middle.

THE DUKE MANSION
Strawberry & Sweet Cream Tart

Yield: 4 servings

- 1¼ cups all-purpose flour
- 3 Tbsp powdered sugar, divided, plus extra for garnish
- 7 Tbsp unsalted butter, softened
- 1 tsp lemon juice
- ½ cup plus 2 Tbsp heavy cream
- zest of 1 lemon
- 8 oz. strawberries, stemmed and quartered
- 4 Tbsp raspberry jelly
- 1 Tbsp water
- 4 sprigs fresh mint, for garnish

Preheat oven to 375°F. Sift together flour and 1½ tablespoons of powdered sugar into a medium bowl. Add butter and lemon juice; knead lightly until a smooth dough is formed. Cover bowl with plastic wrap and refrigerate for 15 minutes.

On a lightly floured surface, roll out dough thinly. Cut dough into 4 pieces. Line 4 (3-inch) tartlet pans with removable bottoms with dough. Put a piece of parchment paper and some dry beans over each piece of dough and bake for 15 minutes (this is called "baking blind"). Remove beans and parchment paper from crusts and bake for 3–5 minutes more, until crusts are golden brown. Cool for 15 minutes, then remove crusts from pans.

Whip cream, remaining 1½ tablespoons of powdered sugar and lemon zest until soft peaks are formed. Spoon whipped cream into crusts. Top with strawberries. Heat jelly with water in a small saucepan over low heat until jelly is melted and combined. Strain jelly mixture through a sieve and cool slightly. Spoon jelly mixture over strawberries to glaze. Dust with powdered sugar and garnish with a sprig of mint to serve.

"Classic" North Carolina Recipes

Ava Gardner Pancakes

Ava Gardner shares her mother's pancake recipe:

Three cups of flour, one teaspoon salt, three teaspoons baking powder, sifted together. Beat three eggs and add to three cups of milk and one tablespoon melted butter. Mix into a smooth batter and cook on a well-greased hot griddle to a nice light brown.

Ava maintained that nothing beats pancakes for breakfast when served piping hot and swimming in butter.

Ava Lavinia Gardner was born on a tobacco farm in Grabtown, North Carolina. At age eighteen, her picture in the window of her brother-in-law's New York photo studio brought her to the attention of MGM, leading quickly to Hollywood and a film contract based strictly on her beauty. Her film career did not bring her great fulfillment, but her looks may have made it inevitable; many fans still consider her the most beautiful actress in Hollywood history.

She studied at Atlantic Christian College (now Barton College) before her movie career. She is buried in Smithfield, North Carolina, home of the Ava Gardner Museum.

Candied Sweet Potatoes

6 sweet potatoes
1½ cups brown sugar
1½ cups cold water
¼ tsp salt

Preheat oven to 350°F. Peel the potatoes and cut in slices ½-inch thick. Place in an iron skillet and add the remaining ingredients. Cover and bake for 40 minutes. Uncover and continue baking for 30 minutes.

North Carolina's hot, moist climate and rich, fertile soil are ideal for cultivating sweet potatoes, making North Carolina the No. 1 state in the United States for sweet potato production. With few natural enemies, pesticides are rarely used and after harvesting, the sweet potatoes undergo a ten-day curing process that converts the starches to sugars. This sweetness intensifies as the sweet potato is cooked, creating the deep caramel flavor.

Aunt Bee's Kerosene Cucumbers

Yield: 6 quarts

Cucumbers
1 bunch dill
6 hot peppers
6 cloves garlic
6 slices onion
6 tsp whole spices
6 lumps alum
1 qt. cider vinegar
2 qts. water
1 cup salt

Wash and dry enough cucumbers for 6 sterilized 1 quart jars. In bottom of jar: some dill, 1 hot pepper, 1 clove of garlic, 1 slice of onion, 1 teaspoon whole spices, small lump of alum and cucumbers. In saucepan combine vinegar, water and salt. Let mixture come to a rolling boil, then pour into the jars. Seal immediately.

Recipe from *Aunt Bee's Mayberry Cookbook* by Ken Beck and Jim Clark

Mayberry is a fictional community in North Carolina that was the setting for two American television sitcoms, *The Andy Griffith Show* and *Mayberry R.F.D.* Mayberry is said to be based on Andy Griffith's hometown of Mount Airy, North Carolina. In the second-season episode of *The Andy Griffith Show*, Aunt Bee makes quarts of inedible pickles to enter in a contest at the county fair. Andy and Barney refer to her pickles as "kerosene cucumbers." The episode often places on "Top Ten Favorite Episodes Lists" of fans and critics.

Calabash North Carolina Shrimp

2	eggs
1	cup whole milk
1	cup all-purpose flour
½	tsp salt
½	tsp black pepper
2	lbs. small shrimp, shelled

In a bowl, beat together the eggs and milk. Add flour, salt, and pepper, and stir until smooth. Dip shrimp in batter; remove and place in hot oil. Fry at 375°F until crisp.

All over the Carolinas, the signs on the restaurants proclaim "Calabash-style seafood." The popular advertising slogan derives from Calabash, N.C., a small fishing village just north of the South Carolina line. There are many views as to the meaning of "Calabash" seafood. Some say it means generous portions; others say it refers to the freshness of the seafood. Still others say it refers to reasonable prices, or meaning a relaxed and homey atmosphere. All agree that you have to go to the real place for the real thing. (Adapted from a *New York Times* article by Steven V. Roberts)

North Carolina BBQ

Barbecue—or BBQ—is very popular in North Carolina. Here it means chopped pork cooked slowly over a hickory fire to take on the smoky flavor. But the key ingredient is the sauce. In eastern North Carolina, the BBQ has a vinegar-based sauce, while in western North Carolina, it has a tomato-based sauce. The recipe here is for the eastern version. BBQ is often served on a bun with sides of coleslaw, hush puppies (fried corn-meal), and baked beans.

2 Tbsp oil	½ tsp salt
2 lb. pork shoulder roast	½ tsp cayenne pepper
½ cup ketchup	cider vinegar as needed
¼ cup apple cider vinegar	hot sauce as needed
1 tsp garlic powder	6 hamburger buns
½ tsp sugar	

Preheat oven to 300°F. Heat the oil over medium heat in a frying pan. Add the pork roast and brown all sides, using the cook's fork to turn the meat (this takes 3 to 5 minutes). Using the fork, remove the meat from the frying pan and place it in a heavy baking dish.

In a saucepan, mix the ketchup, vinegar, garlic powder, sugar, salt, and cayenne pepper. Bring to a boil over medium heat. Pour the sauce over the roast and cover the baking dish. Bake for 2 hours. Spoon the sauce over the meat several times while it cooks. The meat is done when it starts to separate from the bone. Remove the meat from the baking dish and let it cool for about 20 minutes. When the meat has cooled, pull it into bite-sized pieces. Season to taste with additional cider vinegar and hot sauce. Serve on hamburger buns.

Old Time Eastern North Carolina Barbecue Sauce

½ pound butter
3 Tbsp lemon juice (approx. 1 lemon)
1½ Tbsp Worcestershire sauce (preferably Lea & Perrins)
1 Tbsp honey
2 tsp salt
1 tsp black pepper (fresh ground if you have it)
½ cup apple cider vinegar (white will work also)

Once the butter is melted in a saucepan, stir in all but the vinegar and bring to a boil. Remove the pan from the heat, stir in the vinegar, and allow the sauce to cool.

Courtesy Jack and Bob, the Cookin' Cousins at the-greatest-barbeque-recipes.com website.

Western North Carolina Barbecue Sauce

1 cup ketchup
1 cup firmly packed brown sugar
½ cup lemon juice (3 lemons approx.)
3 Tbsp butter
¼ cup minced onion
1 tsp hot pepper sauce
1 tsp Worcestershire sauce

Combine all ingredients in a saucepan, bring to a boil, and simmer for 25–30 minutes.

Courtesy Jack and Bob, the Cookin' Cousins at the-greatest-barbeque-recipes.com website.

Pecan Chicken Salad

         5 cups diced cooked chicken
         1 cup diced celery
         2 cups salad dressing
        1½ cups chopped Red Delicious apples with peel
         2 cups pecan halves
        10   oz. pickle relish
         4 hard-boiled eggs, diced

In large bowl combine chicken, celery, and salad dressing. Add apples, pecans, pickle relish, and eggs. Mix until well blended.

North Carolina produces three to five million pounds of pecans annually. There are approximately 2,000 acres of pecans in North Carolina and most are managed as commercial orchards. North Carolina consistently ranks in the top 10 states in production of new and improved pecan varieties. Georgia leads the nation in pecan production, followed by Texas, then Alabama. An occasional handful of warm, toasted pecans is not only delicious and satisfying, but researchers are finding that they may be as beneficial to your health as cooking with olive oil. Pecans are an excellent source of oleic acid, a fatty acid found in abundance in olive oil. (Recipes courtesy North Carolina Pecan Growers Association)

Summer Squash Pecan Bake

4 cups cooked yellow squash
½ cup onion
2 cans cream of chicken soup
1 cup sour cream
1 cup chopped pecans

Mash squash and combine with onion. Spread in buttered casserole dish. Combine soup and sour cream and spread over squash. Top with pecans. Bake at 400°F for 15 minutes.

Pecan Salad Dressing

3 oz. cream cheese
⅓ cup mayonnaise
⅓ cup orange juice
1 Tbsp lemon juice
1 Tbsp sugar
¼ tsp salt
⅓ cup pecans

Soften cream cheese. Add mayonnaise, juices, sugar, and salt; beat well. Stir in pecans; chill well. Serve on salads.

James Taylor's Corn Pudding

17	oz.	creamed corn
17	oz.	canned corn
8½	oz.	Jiffy Corn Muffin mix
1	cup	sour cream
½	cup	melted unsalted butter

Preheat oven to 300°F. Mix all ingredients together. Bake in a greased casserole dish for 1 hour 40 minutes.

Notes from singer/song writer James Taylor: Add some ground black pepper and a touch of cayenne to make the dish a little less one-dimensional. Not that you could ever make this healthy, but you could substitute low-fat sour cream. I sometimes whip 3 egg whites to make it a little lighter. A little fresh basil or oregano would make the dish a little more interesting—all depends what you are serving with it.

In 1951, when James was three years old, his family moved to what was then the countryside of Chapel Hill, North Carolina, when his father took a job as Assistant Professor of Medicine at the University of North Carolina School of Medicine. They built a house in the Morgan Creek area off of what is now Morgan Creek Road, which was sparsely populated. James would later say, "Chapel Hill, the Piedmont, the outlying hills, were tranquil, rural, beautiful, but *quiet*. Thinking of the red soil, the seasons, the way things smelled down there, I feel as though my experience of coming of age there was more a matter of landscape and climate than people."

Caramel Apple Cinnamon Breakfast Rolls

This dish won 1st Place in the 2011 North Carolina State Fair Apple Recipe Contest. It was submitted by Mary Boury of Knightdale, NC.

1 loaf frozen dough, white or wheat (Rhodes)
2 cups apple slices

Cinnamon filling:
¼ cup soft butter
½ cup sugar
2 tsp cinnamon
⅓ cup chopped walnuts

Caramel Sauce:
18 caramels
2 Tbsp half & half

Preheat oven to 350°F. Thaw bread dough as directed, let rise until doubled, then punch down and let rest 10 minutes. Roll dough out on a 12x8-inch floured board. In a bowl, combine ingredients for the cinnamon filling. Spread filling onto dough. Top with 2 cups very thinly sliced apples such as Honey Crisp. Roll up and slice into 2-inch sections, and place in a greased 9-inch round pan and bake for 30–45 minutes. Place the caramels and half & half in a bowl and microwave until melted. Cool slightly and pour caramel sauce over the rolls.

Country Apple Ham Pizza

This dish won 2nd Place in the 2011 North Carolina State Fair Apple Recipe Contest. It was submitted by Donna Barefoot of Benson, NC.

1 pkg. crescent rolls
1 cup chopped North Carolina apples (red and yellow Delicious)
2 tsp sugar
Dash of salt
3 Tbsp margarine
1 cup large North Carolina Wine Sap apples, sliced
3 Tbsp pecans, chopped
3 Tbsp dried cranberries
4 Tbsp country ham (cooked) and chopped
¼ cup blue cheese, crumbled

Preheat oven to 375°F. Place crescent roll points toward the center of a pizza pan and press together to form crust. Cook chopped apples, sugar, salt and margarine for 5–7 minutes for the sauce. Spread the sauce on the dough. Place sliced apples on top of sauce. Top with pecans, cranberries and ham. Sprinkle with cheese and bake for 20 minutes. Remove from oven and allow to cool for 5 minutes before serving.

Apple Pancetta Frittata

This dish won 3rd Place in the 2011 North Carolina State Fair Apple Recipe Contest. It was submitted by Felica Bogus of Raleigh, NC.

2 large North Carolina apples (such as Mutsu, Fuji, or Gala)
8 large eggs plus 2 large egg whites
1 Tbsp olive oil
3 oz. pancetta, diced
1 medium leek, rinsed well and thinly sliced

Preheat oven to 450°F. Peel, core, and slice apples into ⅛-inch-thick pieces. In a medium bowl, beat together eggs and egg whites. Season to taste with salt and pepper and set aside. Heat the oil in a 12-inch cast iron skillet over medium heat. Sauté pancetta until crisped, about 5 minutes. Remove pancetta with a slotted spoon and reserve. Add leek and sauté an additional 1–2 minutes.

Stir pancetta and leek into beaten eggs and pour eggs into the skillet. Let eggs begin to set, about 1–2 minutes and arrange apples on top of eggs. Place skillet in the top third of the oven and bake until filling is set and top begins to brown, about 20 minutes. Remove from oven and slide frittata onto a cutting board. Let rest 5 minutes before cutting. Serve warm or at room temperature.

Apple Sausage Balls

This dish won Honorable Mention in the 2011 North Carolina State Fair Apple Recipe Contest, using Honey Crisp apples and June Hoop cheese from North Carolina Ashe County Hoop Cheese. It was submitted by Chris Braxton of Durham, NC.

2	cups North Carolina apples, chopped fine
1	cup all-purpose flour
½	tsp baking powder
¼	tsp baking soda
¼	tsp salt
1¾	cups country sausage (16 oz.)
1½	cups sharp cheddar cheese
½	cup smoked Gouda cheese
2	Tbsp maple syrup
⅛	tsp cinnamon
⅛	tsp allspice
⅛	tsp nutmeg (optional)

Preheat oven to 375°F. In a bowl, combine all ingredients, mixing all together with your hands or a mixer to combine. Roll into walnut size balls and place on baking sheet and bake for 20–25 minutes.

Quick Scuppernong Grape Jelly

Yield: 1½ cups

Scuppernong grapes were named after the Scuppernong River in eastern North Carolina, and are the South's version of a traditional grape. They're sweet and juicy with a tough-skinned exterior.

3 lbs. ripe Scuppernong grapes, washed
½ cup sugar
½ tsp powdered pectin

Pull the grapes from their stalks, discarding any that are obviously bruised or damaged, and transfer them to a heavy, non-reactive 2-quart saucepan. Squeeze the grapes through your fingers, slipping their skins off. Mash the pulp slightly with a fork or potato masher. Set the pan on the stove over medium-low heat and cook, stirring occasionally, until the grape juices flow and begin to simmer, about 10 minutes. Simmer 5 minutes. Remove the saucepan from the heat.

Set a conical sieve lined with damp cheesecloth and a jelly bag (or a tamis) over a large mixing bowl and pour the grapes and juices through. Allow the juice to drip into the bowl without pressing on them (which can make the juice cloudy), about an hour. When the pulp and skins lining the cheesecloth and jelly bag look dry and no more juice drips, discard the pulp and skins and pour the juice into a 2-cup glass measure. Cover and refrigerate the juice until it is cold.

Mix the sugar and pectin together in a small bowl and set aside. Turn the chilled grape juice into saucepan and bring it to a simmer over medium-high heat. Pour the sugar mixture into the grape juice and whisk vigorously. Return the juice to a simmer and simmer briskly for 2 or 3 minutes, whisking constantly. Remove the saucepan from the heat and taste for sweetness, adding more sugar if needed. Pour the jelly into a clean, dry 12-ounce wide-mouth jar. Cool until tepid, cover and refrigerate. Keeps refrigerated for several weeks.

Roasted Acorn Squash with Texas Pete® Chipotle Hot Sauce, Honey & Bacon

1 leek, julienned
2 acorn squash, washed thoroughly & cut in half
  Kosher salt & fresh black pepper
4 Tbsp butter, melted
¼ cup Texas Pete® Chipotle Hot Sauce
4 Tbsp brown sugar
¼ cup honey
¼ lb. bacon, thick cut, sliced into lardons, cooked until crispy
¼ bunch scallions, bias cut

Preheat oven to 200°F. Spread the leek in a pan and bake for 12–14 minutes. Remove from oven and turn heat up to 325°F. Season acorn squash with salt and pepper. Place acorn squash flesh side down on lightly oiled baking sheet tray. Roast for 25 to 30 minutes. Remove squash from oven and invert. Combine butter, Texas Pete® Chipotle Hot Sauce, brown sugar, and honey – drizzle atop acorn squash. Roast for an additional 18 to 20 minutes.

To serve: Cut acorn squash into quarters and generously garnish with bacon lardons, chopped scallions and crispy baked leeks.

(Recipe courtesy T.W. Garner Food Company)

Vegetarian Sloppy Joe with Black Beans and Texas Pete® Chipotle Cream

2 Tbsp extra virgin olive oil
2 onions, chopped
4 celery stalks, chopped
1 jalapeño, diced
1 green bell pepper, diced
6 garlic, minced
1 lb. black beans, soaked overnight & cooked
1 cup tomato sauce
3 Tbsp tomato paste
½ cup ketchup
4 tsp Texas Pete® Chipotle Hot Sauce
1 tsp Texas Pete® Hotter Hot Sauce
2 tsp Worcestershire sauce

Heat extra virgin olive oil in a skillet and sauté onions, celery, peppers, and garlic for 6–8 minutes. Add beans, tomato sauce, tomato paste, ketchup, Texas Pete® Chipotle Hot Sauce, Texas Pete® Hotter Hot Sauce, and Worcestershire. Allow to simmer 18–20 minutes.

(Recipe courtesy T.W. Garner Food Company)

Necessity breeds invention. The Great Depression contributed to the creation and sale of Texas Pete hot sauce. T.W. Garner Food Company made various sauces, jams, and jellies. According to historian Milton Ready, the company "found a niche in the competitive barbecue and hot spice market." So, how is it that a tasty red pepper sauce made in North Carolina happens to be named "Texas Pete" anyway? Legend has it that when Sam Garner and his three sons, Thad, Ralph, and Harold, were trying to come up with a brand name for this spicy new sauce they had created, a marketing advisor suggested the name "Mexican Joe" to connote the piquant flavor reminiscent of the favorite foods of our neighbors to the south. "Nope!" said the patriarch of the Garner family. "It's got to have an American name!" Sam suggested they move across the border to Texas, which also had a reputation for spicy cuisine. Then he glanced at son Harold, whose nickname was "Pete" and the Texas Pete cowboy was born.

It all started during the 1920s, when Sam Garner's son, Thad, owned a barbecue restaurant and made a special hot sauce for his establishment. The restaurant failed but the hot sauce and its recipe survived. The family started selling the product in various ways during the 1930s. In 1946, the three brothers formed T.W. Garner Food Company and used the Texas Pete name to produce various sauces, including Worcestershire, wing, and cocktail sauces. The company made such sauces because the sale of Texas Pete was not enough for financial sustainability. During World War II, Texas Pete and other products were sold to the U.S. government as soldier rations.

Since 1942, Texas Pete has been located in Winston-Salem, North Carolina. (Courtesy of the North Carolina History Project)

Moravian Sugar Cookies

Moravian spice cookies are a traditional kind of cookie that originated in the Colonial American communities of the Moravian Church, such as Winston-Salem, NC. The blend of spices and molasses, rolled paper thin, has a reputation as the "World's Thinnest Cookie." They are related to German Lebkuchen; original recipes can be traced back to the eighteenth century.

4½ cups all-purpose flour
¼ tsp baking soda
¼ tsp salt
1 tsp ground cinnamon
½ tsp ground cloves
¼ tsp ground ginger
1 cup packed brown sugar
½ cup butter
½ cup shortening
1½ cups dark molasses
½ tsp distilled white vinegar

In a bowl, mix together flour, baking soda, salt, cinnamon, cloves, and ginger. In a separate bowl, cream together the brown sugar, butter, and shortening. Add to the flour mixture and mix well. Add molasses and vinegar. Mix well. Cover and chill dough overnight.

Preheat oven to 350°F. Roll out a small amount of dough to ⅛ (or less) inch thick. Cut into desired shapes and place on a cookie sheet. Bake for 10 minutes or until light brown.

Quick Moravian Sugar Cake

Yield: 15–20 servings

4 cups biscuit baking mix
¼ cup sugar
¼ cup dry milk (do not mix with water)
½ cup instant potato flakes
2 eggs
3 Tbsp vegetable oil
1 (12-oz.) can beer

Topping:
2 cups light brown sugar
2 Tbsp ground cinnamon
1½ sticks butter, melted

Preheat oven to 350°F. In a bowl, mix together the biscuit mix, sugar, dry milk, and potato flakes. Beat eggs in a large bowl. Add the oil and the beer to the eggs. Combine the dry and the liquid ingredients and stir well. Spread in a 11x17-inch prepared pan (spray with vegetable coating spray and then lightly oil using vegetable oil). Allow to stand for 12–15 minutes. Combine the brown sugar and the ground cinnamon and spread evenly over the top of the batter. With the end of a large wooden spoon, poke holes into batter. Pour melted butter over entire cake making sure the holes are filled. Bake for 20 minutes. Check center for doneness and cook a little longer if necessary.

Carolina Apple Cake

Recipe from the Honorable James B. Hunt, Jr., longest-serving governor in North Carolina's history, serving from 1977–1985 and 1993–2001.

1½ cups cooking oil
2 cups sugar
4 eggs, beaten

Sift together:
3 cups all-purpose flour
1 tsp salt
2 tsp vanilla

Add:
1 tsp baking soda
3 cups diced peeled apples
1 cup chopped nuts

Bake at 350°F for one hour.

Sauce:
1 tsp butter
1 cup brown sugar
¼ cup milk
1 Tbsp vanilla

Simmer sauce for 3 minutes, then pour over warm cake.

Executive Mansion Budget Crunch Brownies

Recipe is from the Honorable Michael F. Easley, 72nd governor of North Carolina, serving from 2001–2009.

Yield: 24 brownies

"The first family likes to serve this dessert during receptions. Since our state is in the process of dealing with a large budget shortfall, we like to stick to the tried and true recipes that can be prepared on a shoestring budget. This recipe fits the bill; we hope you like it."
—*Governor and Mrs. Michael F. Easley*

4	oz. unsweetened chocolate
½	cup (1 stick) unsalted butter
2	cups sugar
4	eggs
1	tsp vanilla extract
1¼	cups all-purpose flour
1	tsp baking powder
1	tsp salt
⅔	cup chopped pecans or walnuts

Preheat oven to 350°F. Grease a 13x9x2-inch baking pan. In a saucepan or microwave, melt chocolate and butter. Blend in sugar, eggs, and vanilla. Then stir in flour, baking powder, salt, and nuts. Pour the mixture into the baking pan. Bake for 30 minutes. Cool slightly, then cut into bars.

Cherokee Bread Pudding

The Cherokees believe that they have always lived in western North Carolina. Finely crafted stone tools and fluted spear-points confirm that ancient people lived here more than 11,000 years ago, at the end of the last Ice Age. Ancient Cherokee tales describe hunts of the mastodons that once foraged through the upland spruce and fir. By 8000 BCE, semi-permanent villages dotted this region. Over the following millennia, the people of these mountains developed settled towns, sophisticated politics and religion, thriving agriculture, stunning pottery, and tremendously effective archery.

2½ cups toasted bread cubes
2½ cups scalded milk
1 cup butter
½ cup sorghum
   pinch of salt
2 eggs, beaten
1 Tbsp pure maple syrup

Preheat oven to 350°F. Lightly grease a casserole dish; add bread cubes. Pour scalded milk over bread; let stand 5 minutes. Heat sorghum, butter, and salt in a saucepan. Gradually pour over bread mixture. Cool. Gradually pour eggs over bread mixture.

Stir in maple syrup. Place dish in a pan of hot water and bake in oven for 50–60 minutes or until firm.

Cherokee Corn Pones

Yield: 8 servings

The Cherokees controlled some 140,000 square miles throughout eight present-day southern states. Villages governed themselves democratically, with all adults gathering to discuss matters of import in each town's council house. Each village had a peace chief, war chief, and priest. Men hunted and fished; women gathered wild food and cultivated "the three sisters"—corn, beans, and squash—cleverly inter-planting them to minimize the need for staking and weeding. This was life that realized harmony with nature, sustainability, personal freedom, and balance between work, play, and praise.

2	cups cornmeal
¼	tsp baking soda
1	tsp salt
½	cup vegetable shortening
¾	cup buttermilk
¾	cup milk
	butter

Combine cornmeal, baking soda, and salt. Cut in shortening until mixture resembles a coarse meal. Add buttermilk and milk, stirring just until dry ingredients are moistened. Form batter into eight ½-inch-thick cakes. Place on a hot greased griddle (400°F). Cook 15 minutes. Turn and cook an additional 15 minutes. Serve hot with butter.

Alphabetical Listing
of Bed & Breakfasts

Recipe Index